Shore
Lines

Shore Lines

Reflections Beside the Wide Water

MARI MESSER

CONARI PRESS

First published in 2004 by Conari Press,
an imprint of Red Wheel/Weiser, LLC
York Beach, ME
With offices at:
368 Congress Street
Boston, MA 02210
www.redwheelweiser.com

Library of Congress Cataloging-in-Publication Data

Messer, Mari.
Shore lines : reflections beside the wide water / Mari Messer.
p.   cm.
ISBN 1-57324-907-6
1. Conduct of life. 2. Seashore—Miscellanea. I. Title.
BJ1595.M47 2004
128—dc22
2004006704

Typeset in Mrs. Eaves and Escrita by Suzanne Albertson

Printed in Canada
TCP
11 10 09 08 07 06 05 04
8   7   6   5   4   3   2   1

*To my dad who first taught
me to love water and my mom
who went along with it.*

CONTENTS

Grateful thanks to:

Jean Fredette for her insightful and thorough feedback, and to the rest of the Writers Group: Isabelle Healy, Gary Vollbracht, Lynn Robbins, Judith Blackburn, and "Mac" McCoy for their valuable comments.

Robyn Heisey, Emily Sauber, Lucine Kasbarian, Laura Lee Mattingly, and Jill Rogers at Red Wheel/Weiser for their patience, professionalism, and unflagging enthusiasm.

Becky Kennedy and Julie Morgan and the countless others at the Public Library of Cincinnati and Hamilton County for helping track hard-to-find resources and answer obscure questions.

Bev Kirk and Radha Chandrashekaran for creative inspiration.

Jane Heimlich for encouragement and support.

Kirk Polking, Barb Anderson, and Linda Walker for help in moments of desperation.

Computer whiz Lori Nichols for more help in moments of desperation.

Eve Haverfield at *Turtletime* for insights into the lives of sea turtles.

Donna Dahlke and Alberta Addy of the once-upon-a-time Beach House, Dan Weaver at Seabird, and Annalies Johnson at Blue Water Beach Club for their hospitality over the years.

Wading In: An Introduction

Year after year I return to the seabeach to hunt for treasure that can be captured in words and packed along with damp beach towels and faded sunhat to bring home. As tools, I use only a fast-flowing pen and a spiral notebook with a sea scene on the cover. Most of the regulars where I stay have become used to seeing me, alone under the eaves, writing. I'm a fixture like the blue heron standing ankle deep in shallow water, staring out to sea, left to wade in unbothered solitude.

The things I write about happen in the subtle space between everyday life and imaginal life, between beach and sea. I write as everyone's resident solitary, and no one ever asks me what I'm putting down. To those around me, I've become as familiar as the fisherman, sitting on his stool at water's edge, casting.

Writers are like wind-up toys. Set us down anywhere and we begin to scribble. Many of us, you'll notice, scribble better near water. John Masefield, Annie Dillard, Anne Morrow Lindbergh, Tolstoy,

Hemingway, Thoreau, all revered the Big Water. They are not alone. Like beached hermit crabs naked in the sun, most of us crave water.

In the absence of Big Water, any water will do. Water invites solitary reflection. On a closet shelf, I've stored stacks of journals written in watery places: river, fountain, quarry, lake. The notebooks literally drip with wateriness. Over time, I've filled a heap of notebooks with sea stories written at different times and in different places along a hundred-mile stretch of Florida Gulf Coast. They were composed on-the-spot, largely as an attempt to preserve the experience. But mostly these stories were put down as a way to enter solitude and save in some way a drop or two of seawater to bring home.

Even when these notebooks began to pile high, I had no notion that they would ever see life beyond their handwritten pages. But one day my friend, Karen, who had injured her leg and now hobbled around with a cast, called to say she couldn't get out and wanted company. Would I bring something to read to her as she reclined, foot up, to listen? I would. I'd just returned from a trip where I'd filled a whole new notebook, and I was eager to read. We sat on her deck in the cool shade of poplars and maples, and I read to the cadence of a stream burbling below. Afterward, Karen said, "You ought to do something with these stories." Later I shared the writings with others and they agreed.

That's how *Shore Lines* came to be. In the pages that follow, you're invited to join me in a sabbatical by the sea, a deep dive for sunken treasure that interweaves myth, fact, and moment-to-moment experience of the seabeach. I hope these sea stories will stir your wonderings and rememberings, and inspire you to explore your own inner sea-space.

To some, taking time for reflection may seem like selfish indulgence in the uncertainty and upheaval of today's frenetic, fast-moving world. But perhaps now, more than ever, we need just such a respite, a chance to restore balance and clarity, refresh, renew, and look more closely and with jolly good humor at ourselves and our world. We need to *go* apart when there's danger we may come apart.

If you can't get to the sea, I urge you to sit beside a fountain in a park; seek out a river, a lake, even a puddle for your reflection. Or simply come along on an imaginal sojourn beside the sea as you read these pages. Go deep. Fling your fishing line wide and let the hook go down. When you feel a tug, pull up the line to net some surprising new shimmery thing you've never seen before. Something to bring back to your everyday life when your time by the sea is over.

I

The Beach Between
Time on the Edge

It takes considerable courage to stay as long as
needed in a place between, and it requires a degree
of holy foolishness to seek one out.
—THOMAS MOORE, *Neither Here Nor There*

You don't arrive all-at-once at the beach. Fresh off a plane from the still-frigid north, you pad into the bright gleam of sun on white sand like a bear emerging from a winter's nap, squinting and snuffling the air so strangely alive with the scent of warm awakenings. It takes a while to adjust to the change, to settle in, to feel at home in this place between.

I have left my big bearcoat and mufflers at home and shuffle out to the beach, muffled now only in sea air and unaccustomed sun on my shoulders.

These first hours always feel like a jolting leap from hibernation into wakefulness. Suddenly surrounded by sea and solitude, I feel, as Anaïs Nin once wrote, as if my skin has been peeled away and every subtle seabreeze touches deep. In this state of betweenness, I try to get my bearings. My squinty eyes begin to open to the ocean's wide horizon.

Out near the water, a young father is teaching his son to fly a red, diamond-shaped kite in the high wind. With great patience, the man holds the kite while the boy tugs it into flight. Each time, the kite nosedives into sand. But the father keeps picking it up, and the boy husbands it into the air again and again. At last the boy seems to get the hang of it and manages to yank the string to pull the paper diamond aloft over the sea.

"Let it out!" father shouts. "Let all the string out—let it go!" The youngster lets the wand of string unroll as the kite soars higher and higher to become a distant red patch against the blue sky.

That's what you do here, I think, as I watch father and son stand together beside the wide water, looking up at the red-winged kite, ascending. You reel out some long-restrained part of yourself. Let it take flight over breaking waves. Let it find its own height.

Mustering that part of you into flight takes patience. The thing that was born to fly has been forgotten for a while, packed away on a closet shelf, perhaps, among the beach towels.

So it is with great care that you tug it aloft and let it have its head. You coax. Cajole. Shepherd it into the air over the sea. After a few tries it remembers how to fly again, to see beyond the horizon's edge. From high up, the flying thing can telegraph other realities along its string. It can send dreams of that far-off place where words are lost and thoughts dissolve of dishes left unwashed in the kitchen sink.

Where land meets sea, solitude unfolds. This wrinkle in time materializes on the edge between familiar, distracted unravelings of everyday life and unplumbable depths of the vast ocean. The shore of these Gulf Coast keys defines the solid ground of the ordinary world—earthy, substantial, firm. Its sandy lip contains the unruly sea. Like a basin, it holds. It holds while the sea beyond indulges its nature: free, emotional, fierce, playful, irrational, wild. These two—sea and beach—live in continual struggle, like the wild and tamed sides of ourselves.

The sea is nearly the only place on our planet that we haven't completely mapped, explored, subdivided, and conquered. Mostly, it remains a mystery. As my friend Howard says, "The ocean is profound because it is unknowable. Subject to its own internal laws and rhythms, the human world must accommodate it rather than impose upon it." Howard knows a thing or two about oceans because he's spent some time photographing and getting to know them. He sees the edge between land and sea as the bridging point where opposites meet.

The seabeach is fulcrum. It keeps known and unknown in balance, which is why I seek its companionship. It provides a way to right my leaning life. With regularity, I am as out-of-kilter as the Tower of Pisa, tilting. I keep getting caught up in a treadmill of to-dos, forgetting the importance of allowing time to reflect. The seabeach puts me right again. It reorganizes the scatter of my life. How this works, I haven't the foggiest notion.

Too much world dries you out, gets you stuck. Too much introspection leaves you fogged and disconnected. Both extremes are unhealthy. Whenever there is an imbalance between two poles, life becomes lopsided. In our modern mechanized rush, the pole that's most often neglected, given short shrift, is the one that connects with the enigma inside.

The balance between the two sides is constantly changing, just as the edge of the seabeach is constantly changing—eaten away and restored again by current and storm. I come to the water's edge to set things straight, to add to the side that weighs short. My way to find my own equilibrium is to sit beside the sea until the inside begins to clear. You may be able to do this just as well, if not better, in some other place: in the thin air of pine mountains, in the seclusion of cloistered walls, or wherever your own place of incubation may be.

Once you're in your refuge, you may feel the urge to connect the flying thing inside you to the ground, like a kite anchored by its string. My way is writing. You may be drawn to creating images on canvas, trading insights with friends, practicing simple mental mulling, or some other means of processing. Reverie begs for expression. It hangs onto your sleeve like a child intent on having its way, and it won't let go until you wrestle with your innards long enough to make the unknown, known. Solitude provides the arena.

Solitude by the sea takes some getting used to. You wade in little by little. In my case, I'm always and continually out of practice, uncomfortable at first with empty hours. Awkward, as if I've never done this harebrained thing before. It's a feeling I have every time, no matter how often I seek time away from the everyday. Solitude always brings up the familiar love-hate relationship I have with being alone in unstructured time.

I remember my first and only silent retreat, driving two hundred miles to a Catholic convent on a hill miles from anywhere. Arrived and installed in my austere cell, I felt panic closing in. There was just me, a cot, a desk, a straight chair, and one window. No TV. No one to talk to. How could I survive a whole week of silence? Mentally, I repacked my bags and imagined struggling through the immense wood retreat house door, calling back: "Sorry. Family emergency. Have to go home."

But I didn't go. I stayed. And soon, sooner than I would have imagined, solitude closed in again, but in a friendly, welcoming way. As the week unfolded, I was surrounded by silent others—the biker type with long tangled hair tied back with a leather thong, the freckle-faced nun in Birkenstock sandals and shorts, the couple from Indianapolis, holding hands. Silence began to grow around us. It was the kind of silence that had a lot to say to us, and we listened.

"You have to remember how solitude works," someone told me when I revealed my awful panic brought on the first day of that trip. "You have to shift gears," he said, "and allow the mud to settle." Yes. The mud—the residue of life in the world—has to be given time to sink to the bottom, to become unimportant, at least for awhile, till things get clear. It's a process of always having to relearn how to reconnect with the other side.

And so I've come to expect resistance and let it settle itself out. I help it along by making my pen move across a page, even if it feels as stiff and dead as driftwood. At first, it moves stubbornly, belligerently, against the resistance. It writes stuff like:

I don't feel like writing. I'm only doing this to record the passing days so I'll know when to go home. It hasn't come yet, this sense of connection. Maybe because I haven't settled in yet, or settled down. No matter how hard I try, it comes when it's darned good and ready.

The frustration in these words reflects what many actually feel when they first step off the spinning world into solitude. It takes no small leap of faith to believe that a time apart will actually lead to a real sense of connection with the beach, the sea, and that other elusive Something we often tend to ignore.

Maxim Gorky, the Russian writer, described such a connection when he penned a verbal sketch of his compatriot, Leo Tolstoy, who had settled into solitude beside the sea at Gaspra. He observed Tolstoy in a wrinkled gray suit and crumpled hat, sitting with his head in his hands at the water's edge,

> the wind blowing the silvery hairs of his beard through his fingers: he was looking into the distance, out to sea, and the little greenish waves rolled up obediently to his feet and fondled them as if they were telling something about themselves to the old magician . . . He, too, seemed to me like an old stone come to life, who knows all the beginnings and the ends of things.

Tolstoy had come to spend time by sea as a way to reconnect with an elusive but essential dimension in himself. He came, as I do, with hopes for reunion.

A woman I know said recently, "If you like being *by* the sea, you should try being *on* the sea." I thought about what she said. But, no. To me the sea is too untamed, too limitless, to imbibe all in one gulp. The boundary between land and sea provides a *temenos,* a safe haven where inner and outer, wild and tamed, imaginative and reasoned parts of ourselves can make contact with each other. The seabeach mediates between warring opposites.

The beach provides a containing framework. It gives substance, defines—even confines—solitary meanderings. Going inside oneself is too risky without a safety line to lead the way back. We may need, as Lucy Irvine wrote in *Castaway,* a "pattern of conformity" to define our boundaries. Without such boundaries we can really be *at sea,* lost in vastness. "When the pattern of conformity is set, then you can see where your freedoms lie," Irvine said.

Framework first, then freedom. On days when a misty haze hangs over the sea like a gauze curtain, smudging boundaries between water and sky, I need such a point of reference all the more. Weighted by damp, warm air and groggy with sunshine, I drowse in the timeless morning where clocks cease to tell the truth and only shortening shadows prove the sun's rising.

It's just such a state that inspires the urge to reflect and to jot down what bubbles up as a result. The sea serves as catalyst. But being near the sea soon becomes a passion, and, like drinking salt water, the more you consume, the thirstier you get.

This passion for water drove me to seek one island after another, never the same one twice, yet never the one that provided exactly what I was looking for. It took years and years of islands of every size, description, and national origin to finally make me realize that I was searching for communion with the sea by traveling to its every habitat, thinking *there* I would find its essence and that essence would reveal The Big Secret. If I could decipher such a secret, I thought, then I would know something really worth knowing. So I scuttled down high cliffs to the South China Sea, slept by the roaring ocean in St. Maarten, watched the tide come in on Harbor Island, and wandered lonely stretches along the water's edge on Andros. In the end, I came back empty, the Secret still stubbornly, maddeningly untold.

What was I thinking? When I was in the sea's presence, the Secret loomed large, even if I couldn't put it into words. But when the plane winged off for home, I couldn't remember the song the sea had hummed. The Secret was gone.

So I kept coming back for reunion, for another chance to get it right. Over time I learned what others have figured out long ago: The sea is experience. You can't take it with you. You can only hold a conversation with its immensity right here, right now in this solitary place between land and sea. You come to the water's edge, plotz yourself down, and wait. Wait like the boy and his father, patiently, for the wind to be just right and for the red kite to rise over the water, while all along a voice inside you calls, "Let it out! Let it all out!"

If you show up time after time to prove your intentions, the sea will begin to talk to you—to tell you, not The Big Secret, but little ones. Little ones that like the Big One, can't be translated into words. And, like the Big One, these secrets won't make you a magnate in the stock market. They won't make you better looking or richer or a more interesting conversationalist. They won't do a darned thing for you that the world will want to remark about, if indeed the world is aware of any change at all in you.

But if you have, as Thomas Moore says, the "holy foolishness" to seek solitude beside the sea and the courage to endure the uncertainties of being on the edge, you may find a satisfying place for your soul to soar, and in the soaring, to renew itself again.

2

Neptune's Nudge
Remembering Our Origins

For all its tough-minded stance, and despite the elegance of its mathematical formulas, science has not solved but only postponed the question of the origin of things.

—DAVID MACLAGAN, *Creation Myths*

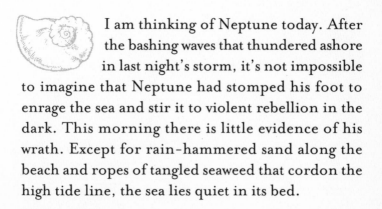 I am thinking of Neptune today. After the bashing waves that thundered ashore in last night's storm, it's not impossible to imagine that Neptune had stomped his foot to enrage the sea and stir it to violent rebellion in the dark. This morning there is little evidence of his wrath. Except for rain-hammered sand along the beach and ropes of tangled seaweed that cordon the high tide line, the sea lies quiet in its bed.

At this early hour, the sea god is likely sleeping it off. Regretting, perhaps, his nighttime carousing by snoozing beneath the calm water. I can imagine him there, cozy in his coral castle, his chariot parked outside among the tall stands of kelp, its seahorse team out of harness, resting with their tails curled under them, glad to have brought the boss home safely.

I think about such things as I hike the mile or so up the beach to the end of Hickory Island. Here waits a quiet cove I visit most mornings. Even on busy weekends, the place is usually empty, offering an immediate sense of peace and containment. Formed by huge piles of coral, shell, and cement, the walls of the cove were once part of a breakwater that protected the properties at island's end where the beach had eroded over time.

A few years ago, when the beach had completely washed away, the shore was "renourished." Huge, rusting pipes were strung together like hoses from a colossal vacuum cleaner, to transport sand from the distant ocean bottom to the beach. It took a couple of months. After that, the breakwater was dismantled and hauled, chunk by chunk, to the tip of the island where it shelters a semicircular cove. Inside the cove lies a small strip of beach, separate from the longer stretch that edges the rest of the island. Little do I know that today, in this cove, before the sun clears the tall pines, I will meet up with a real live Neptune.

As I arrive at the end of the island and skitter down a high dune to get to the cove, it's clear why no one comes here. Sand fills my shoes. It burns my backside where I've sledded the steep incline. I'm relieved the place is empty. All alone except for an absurd contingency of wildlife that congregates on the coral reef or at the water's edge, I watch ibis, egret, heron— even a dead stingray, its bulbous gray body washing in and out on the rills.

Today the sea is green. Not green like fir trees or like new leaves in April, but green like old jade with a tinge of brown. Daily, even hourly, the colors change. The water is, as Nathan Altman wrote in *Sacred Water,* a living substance, "marvelous, magical, and sacred." On any day, you can observe its surface. What's going on below is anybody's guess.

And I can't help guessing. Earlier imaginations saw the underwater world as a hangout for Neptune and his cohorts. The story goes that in ancient times three brothers got together to divide the world among themselves. Neptune, the name Romans gave to the Greek god Poseidon, demanded kingship of the waters. His two brothers claimed sky and underworld.

Originally, Neptune ruled over rivers. The wisdom of the time saw the earth as flat, surrounded by a wide, mysterious ocean-river that wrapped around the known world. What went on beyond the ocean-river, no one knew. Seamen feared they could sail off the edge of the imagined border of water they called Oceanus.

The Greek epic poet Homer, who lived in the eighth century B.C., drew an early world map that looked a lot like a thin pizza with the ocean as its surrounding crust. Contained within the narrow border of ocean were regions with names like "The Borders of Night" and "The Entrance to the Infernal Regions." Obviously, Homer didn't have satellite access to aid his mapping. But he did have an enormous imagination.

It was likely that just such an imagination led early Romans and Greeks to envision the population of the underwater world as looking remarkably like *us.* Having little knowledge of the unexplored world, they created myths to explain the unexplainable. Neptune, a central figure in these myths, was seen as a patriarch, nearly human, but with greatly exaggerated powers.

The ruler of the sea flaunted those powers. On a whim, he could shake his trident to cause furious storms or wave it like a wand to calm disturbed waters. The instrument, which he held upright like a staff, was believed to have supernatural powers. Its three sharply pointed prongs represented the teeth of a sea monster. If you're beginning to get the idea that Neptune wasn't exactly a friendly kind of guy, you're most likely right. Forced to live far from sunlight and dry land, who wouldn't get cranky?

The upshot was, Neptune's temper tantrums kept ordinary humans in a state of fear. As the myth unfolded, the sea god took on the ambivalence and the frightening mystery of the sea itself. Neptune, with his unpredictable rages, was a god to be shunned. He represented to those early minds all that we fear and detest in ourselves, all that we cast into the deep sea where it works without our knowing, in the dark.

Because of these early beliefs, it took a long while before anyone became friends with the sea. Even as recently as the early 1800s, the ocean was seen as ugly and even threatening. Fishermen, having experienced the fury of the sea up close, usually lived at the back of their houses to stay as far away from the water as they could. The sea was apparently not something they wanted to commune with on their time off.

Today, almost everywhere you look, you'll see vast human rookeries that crowd the seabeach. Could it be that we are edging closer and closer to what some scientists say is our place of origin? Are we homesick for the waters they say we came from? I wonder.

I wonder about these things as four white ibis drop from the sky to wade in the shallows of the cove. They turn their heads sideways, so they can see me out of their red eyes that look like a sunburst or a bruise about to develop into a shiner. These four must have inspired the term "strange birds." Their stiff-legged strut, their downward-curving beaks that look like a swashbuckler's scimitar, their spindly legs, all conspire to help them live up to the title. Soon they wing off, their legs trailing, streamlined, behind.

With the birds' departure, the cove feels deserted. There is just the jing of crickets in a clump of sea oats on the ridge behind me. And in the coral rock, seawater whispers an echoey sigh as it hisses through crevices and trickles out again.

Out to sea, there's nothing but a broad expanse of green. I squint my eyes and try to see clear to Texas. I can't. There is only endless ocean spreading precisely to the edge of the sky. Still, I imagine that the other coast lies somewhere out there beyond the broad water. It is this water, this seawater, that widens. It stretches the imagination and puts to sleep, at least temporarily, the internal thinking machine that incessantly calculates, demands answers, and shoves each thing into its proper and neat little box.

The vast sprawl of shifting, moving watery horizon triggers a return to origins. Mind layers peel away, backward. We return to beginnings. This going back reminds me of what Albert Camus said in *Notebooks,* that "every summer morning on the beach feels like the first morning of the world." We return to a primal brain that rubs a sleepy eye and begins to wake. Unconfined by the box we live in, the box we work in, and the four-wheeled box we drive between the two, our thoughts drift out over the water like a gull cruising air currents.

In such a state of mind, strange things can happen. Real and unreal melt together in the warm mist of the seabeach. Myth reemerges. It connects us to the "missing link" in human evolution that some scientists say is missing because we have spent some unknown era as residents of an underwater world. A world where Neptune reigns.

Some evidence points to our watery origins. We

once were, of course, each of us and all, inhabitants of the inner sea of the womb. Here we drifted and dreamed ourselves into being. And then, around the sixth month, something odd happened that seems to prove where we came from. Our bodies became covered with fine hair called *lanugo,* usually shed before birth or shortly after. What's interesting about this fetal fur coat, one theory goes, is the way the hair grows. It grows in the same way water passes over a *swimming body!* Could it be that at some point in our evolution we were water creatures? Could Neptune have been the mayor of our village?

I think about these connections as I remember what I read about the six-foot-long *Coelacanth,* a rare fish known affectionately as "old fourlegs." The creature is part of a family of "Dinofish," the rest of the clan having succumbed to extinction sixty-five million years ago. There are scientists who say this fish appears to be a distant relative of the *Eusthenopteron,* who in some circles is credited with growing legs and stumping ashore some 360 million years ago. One theory contends that this fish and its kin were the ancestors of all landlubber animals, including us! Just think. Neptune, "the earth shaker," might once have lived in the coral castle next door to ours.

Thinking about the god of the sea has lured me into a Neptune state of mind. Watery. Aware that more than eighty-five percent of me, of you, of everybody, is water, I am filled with vague imaginings, as vast as the green water that stretches empty beyond the cove. In this Neptune state, my mind floats out over the water, gliding low like a pelican, winging.

Then, suddenly surfacing from reverie, I see them. Huge footprints in the sand. Had they been there all along and I hadn't noticed? Obviously made by enormous bare feet, the footprints aren't unusual in themselves. What makes them remarkable is that they seem to emerge right out of the sea. No other prints deface the virgin sand of the cove except these that trek inland from the water's edge. I imagine some sea god, green hair wet and streaming, his eyes a-sparkle, skin shiny dark, coming up out of the calm water. I imagine he is Neptune, carrying his trident like a spear, drawn by some irresistible urge to leave the deep and venture onto dry land.

From the size of his footprints, I'd guess him to be well over six feet tall, a height befitting a sea god. The image so arrests my imagination that I'm astonished to see a distant figure materialize from behind coral boulders surrounding the cove. Seemingly, he has emerged from the sea. The strikingly human-looking Neptune stands up to his waist in quiet green water. He has waded into view several hundred feet away, just past the edge of the coral heap. He's as surprised to see me as I am to see him.

For a moment, I think I'm seeing Neptune suddenly rising from the sea. Perhaps it's my stare, transfixed by his brown body, bare from the waist up, and shining with sea water, that makes him turn, like an animal startled, to disappear again behind the pile of coral rock. In the instant before he vanishes from sight, I see him toss a bait net over a tanned shoulder. So much for mystery. So much for a green-haired Neptune emerging from the sea.

And yet. And yet. The infinite variety of creatures, humans included, that inhabit the seabeach and the sea itself seem no stranger than those early mythic characters. Both tickle curiosity. They set the mind to wondering how we got here. In whose immense imagination did these odd beings, imaginary and real, originate?

Neptune isn't talking.

3

The Night the Sea Stars Came Out
Becoming Part of the Rainbow

We are cups, constantly and quietly being filled. The trick is, knowing how to tip ourselves over and let the beautiful stuff out.

—RAY BRADBURY

At dusk, the sky over the sea turns orange like a banked fire. Several of us who have gathered to watch the sunset are amazed to see that stars have come out on land as well as in the sky. Someone has pulled the plug in the ocean's unfathomable bathtub, and at low tide a sandbar emerges a dozen yards from shore. It is splotched with nine-armed starfish big as dinner plates. Abandoned by the receding tide, the shy sea stars burrow firmly into the sand. They camouflage themselves with bits of debris until their daisy shapes almost disappear.

Piled high over the darkening sea, red, pink, yellow, and mauve clouds reflect their blurry, cotton candy shapes on the damp sandbar. At the edge that borders the open sea, waves turn gentle. Between sandbar and shore lies a quiet temporary pool, clear enough even in declining light to reveal a nine-armed sea star fingering along its bottom.

It's a rare thing, this emergence of the sea stars. I've seen it only twice in all the years I've been coming here to the Gulf Coast of Florida. Rarity invites wonder. It attracts us. It causes us to notice. Contrarily, when something happens predictably, interest evaporates. We've become immune, for instance, to wondering about heavenly stars, coming out as they do every cloudless night. Hardly ever do we look up unless some sensation draws our attention: a comet shower, a rare eclipse. Is it possible to wonder about everyday miracles?

Emerson would have said "yes." In *Nature,* he wrote: "If the stars should appear one night in a thousand years, how would men believe and adore, and preserve for many generations the remembrance of the City of God which had been shown."

Maybe, in the same way, the sea stars have come out to restore our wonder.

But the earthly "City of God" is short-lived. Out on the sandbar, shadows barely recognizable as human forms stoop low and straighten and stoop again. The dark figures, stark against the burn of sundown, scour their way from one end of the sandbar to the other, plucking live stars from their beds and heaping them in piles to take ashore.

I know what will happen. I've seen it all before. Live stars will be spread out on the wood picnic tables in tomorrow's hot sun to dry. The stars, of course, will not live long. And as fragile as they are, they will likely lose an arm or two and, ultimately, the collectors will leave them behind. Even the intact creatures will start to smell of death after a while, and no one wants to tuck that reminder in a suitcase. I remember a conch shell I once aimed to take home from a remote island. It taught me a lesson about such smells.

A ragtag group of youngsters was cleaning conchs at Driggs Hill Dock on Andros one morning when I happened to bicycle past. The boys were after the conch meat, a valuable commodity in the islands. After the flesh was removed, they left dozens of empty shells the size of Rembrandt war helmets for the ocean to take out when it willed. I hauled one of the freshly gutted queen conchs back to my room. In a few days, the smell nearly drove me out and I returned the shell to the sea. The experience cured me of collecting anything living or newly dead.

Still thinking about the island episode, I wade out to see what's happening on the sandbar. There are not so many sea stars now. Gatherers have snatched them up, leaving only cookie-cutter shapes in the sand. A dozen dark figures continue to work their way along the strip. They capture their prey silently, relentlessly, in the dying light. The piles of sea stars grow.

The stars remind me of a book I found years ago one rainy morning when I raided the musty shelves in a motel office and returned to my room with an armload of reading. You never know what you're likely to find, since the books are left behind by other people. This time, among the yellowing, salt-stained paperbacks, I discovered Loren Eiseley's *The Star Thrower*.

Eiseley tells of a mythic experience along these same westward-gazing shores. Every day, on his walks along the beach, he encounters the shell collectors and the boiling pots in which "the beautiful voiceless things were being boiled alive." As he walks on, he comes to a deserted part of the beach where he sees— at least in his mind's eye—a Thrower of stars, larger than life, silhouetted against a rainbow in the sky. The Thrower flings sky stars, sowing life on an immensely larger scale. Eiseley, too, joins in by casting the sea stars at his feet back into the sea in much the same way the Thrower casts stars in the upper realms "for the uses of life." And, he says, along with the stars, he casts himself as forfeit.

What does it mean to cast oneself as forfeit? I looked up the word. It means to relinquish, give over—even surrender. How can you give yourself to life, throw yourself to the winds in a spirit of total consent to whatever the Thrower, the Great Spirit, has in store? All my life I've hesitated on the brink of total commitment. I've held back, been too careful, reluctant to risk, afraid to give everything to the process. "Go at your life with a broadaxe," Annie Dillard advises. Left to my own devices, I usually go at mine with a toothpick.

Solitaries like me prefer to be observers. Maybe that's why so many of us become writers. We can reflect on life without actually living it, flat out. In this way we can experience, vicariously, other people's adventures—sometimes even fictional people's adventures—and yet avoid throwing ourselves as forfeit, completely and unconditionally, into life.

Fortunately for us deliberate wallflowers, life has other ideas. Life itself flings us into adventures we never imagined (or in some cases might not have wanted to imagine). We're carried along on the tide's surge, whether we want to go or not. It's better, I expect, if the going has our full consent.

With my feet imbedded like the tentacles of a starfish in the wet sand of the sandbar, I try to imagine Eiseley's Thrower with the immense rainbow at his back. But all I see is a wide sky heaped with purple clouds growing darker and darker. Water begins to trickle over my toes. The tide is coming in again. Atlantis is submerging.

Only a few stars remain, and the rest leave only their sad imprints, like concave sunbursts in the sand. Without thinking, I bend over and pick up one of the survivors. At first I'm repelled by its spiky feel in my hand. (Their resemblance to giant spiders can't be missed.) In fact, there's really nothing very endearing about them. They have no faces, no child-like pouty mouths like the stingrays, no sweet Dumbo expressions like the manatees. How can you relate to a creature with nine prickly purple arms, no head, and no brain? But then, I'm slipping into the trap, am I not, of wanting to make the thing human—or at least loveable?

Without thinking, still, I toss the star far out to sea. The tide begins to sweep over the sandbar in a gull-wing pattern of rainbow ripples, as inky blue and iridescent as the inside of an abalone shell. I start to fling the rest of the stars, one by one. I like them more with every throw. As I heave them out to sea, I remember that they have rudimentary eyes at the end of each tentacle, and even though they can see only light and dark in a myopic way, I sense they may *know*. They may feel my fingers on their hard, knobby skin and realize that as they are being helped to survive, I am making an effort to love them. Is it possible to love an ugly creature simply because it's alive and has been created by some high power with a wayward sense of humor? I try.

"We must learn to love the unlovely," said a training instructor long ago, to a group of us college students who were summer interns at the Elgin State Mental Hospital. We were gathered around shabby tables in the basement occupational therapy room, listening raptly. It was the first time I'd heard such a revolutionary idea. It went against everything I thought at the time about the handsome and the popular being the only ones worth loving. We were, the instructor said, not only to learn to love the unlovely. We were to *show* it by acts of kindness to the ones who had lost their way in the labyrinths of mental illness.

In the months that followed, those of us who were about to return to college tried to lavish our love on the man who smelled like ripe sweat socks and talked to people who walked through walls, on the woman who wanted to be a man and smoked like an industrial chimney, and on all the others. We flung ourselves, full tilt, into spreading kindness for "the uses of life." Sometimes we were successful, sometimes not.

When any of us slipped up, we'd get reminded of our purpose. After a while a funny thing happened. The patients began to respond. Not all of them. Not the one who sat silent, rolling triangles of wallpaper into beads, day after day. Not the one who hid under the stairs because she feared the building would collapse. But some. Their response egged us on. We learned a gem of a lesson that summer.

Despite remembering all these years about loving the unlovely, there have been large and long lapses in my doing. I try now to redeem the lapses by tossing the remaining stars at my feet.

Collectors begin to retreat to shore, sloshing through the tidepool, their arms filled with live stars. The returning tide moves in over the sandbar to cover the odd-shaped graves. As I toss the last star into the sea, I'm left with the thought that some acts lead toward life and some lead away.

I have not always, maybe not even usually, been on the side of life. Beyond that, beyond regrets, I have only questions. How can we take a stand "for the uses of life"? Contribute to each others' well-being, create something beautiful or useful, solve a problem, learn, teach? How can we nurture the life-enhancing forces and discourage the life-destroying ones? Where do we stand in the great complexity of things, and how can we honor and help preserve that complexity, whether we find its constituents endearing or not, useful or not?

It can be frightening to "fling yourself as forfeit," to give yourself over to a greater purpose and to make a stand for life. But it's also exhilarating to fling your star to the wind, into the unpredictable, letting some force outside you take over, giving up control, giving yourself over, trusting life to help you leap the hurdles, trusting the Thrower to guide your trajectory so you'll go the way you're meant to go and, ultimately, get to where you're meant to be.

After a while you begin to see your starpath. You know more and more surely where you're going. But you don't plan your way, every step, willfully. Instead, you live along into it like you do when you and a friend are batting a beachball back and forth over a net: you base your moves on how the ball comes over. Your strategy changes minute by minute as you fling yourself into the process.

Is it a coincidence that we stand, as Eiseley did, on this same wave-worn coast, surrounded by stars? Stars above. Stars below at our feet. I wish he were here to answer the questions I wonder about. All I have is the memory of a passage in a now much-read book that tells how the author joined the Thrower, hurling live stars back into the sea—"for the uses of life." The Thrower is no longer alone, Eiseley writes: "After us there will be others. We were part of the rainbow."

4

Elephants of the Sea
A Close Encounter

*Nobody can drown in the ocean of reality who
voluntarily gives himself up to it.*

—HENRY MILLER

 As a very small child, long before I met
up with the elephants of the sea, I had an
odd fantasy. I imagined that we human
beings did not experience life firsthand as most
seemed to think. Instead, I visualized us wired to a
master switchboard that simulated experiences by
means of electrical impulses. (I'm sure this image
was inspired by old movies of switchboard operators
plugging in calls as they came. How such an apparatus worked was a mystery to me and all the more
fascinating.)

So I pictured us linked up to the master control box. But I kept wondering in a vague, offhand, child-mind way: was there another existence beyond the wires? A richer, fuller life that we didn't know about? If there was, I was determined even then to find it.

At the time, if anyone would have asked, I probably couldn't have expressed what I was searching for. The thoughts were far too wispy to put into words. I sensed even as a kid that to catch in the act this other way of existing had to do with never letting my attention lapse. I was Sherlock Holmes. Nothing was going to escape my notice.

When I licked a chocolate ice cream cone, tasting its dusky sweetness, I was trying to experience "beyond the wires." So, too, with other ordinary sensations: smelling gasoline when my dad refueled our tan Plymouth sedan at the station, feeling the smooth cut velvet on the maroon living-room chair that no one ever sat in, and listening to twittering sparrows huddled together on a bare branch outside my bedroom window.

These childhood experiences drew me early on toward a passionate quest for the Real that I was certain lay beyond the wired world. Ultimately that quest led me to water, as naturally as a camel seeks an oasis.

There was no ocean near my home in a small land-locked town in Illinois, but I made regular pilgrim-ages on my bike to rivers, ponds, and creeks. I brought along a day's sustenance: a brown paper bag filled with peanut butter sandwiches on fluffy white Silvercup bread, a wax paper sack of salty potato chips, and a bottle of tangy Orange Crush. Thus supplied, I'd cycle to some body of water, sit by its banks, munch lunch, and pedal home, sated with peanut butter and satisfyingly reconnected to my watery soul.

Little did I realize then that my early fantasy of being wired to a console would one day be lived out—not just by me, but by everyone in our modern age of personal machines. Are we not, today, in many ways connected to a master board that substitutes for real experience? Do we not react as if what we experience by way of our wires, our movies, computers, and TV screens, is real? (Notice how your stomach clenches when you see an electronic image of an attacker looming in the dark of a TV or movie set. Isn't this the same reaction you'd have to the real thing?) Hooked up to our contraptions, fantasy and reality merge. Eventually, the unreal seems real.

Wires plug us into distorted reality in many ways. Electric blankets fool us into believing we live in a place of perpetual summer. Air conditioning lulls us into thinking that summer is cooler than it really is. Clocks click us into arbitrary time. We set them forward or back depending on the season and man-made daylight saving time, regardless of how our bodies respond to being jerked back and forth. And, of course, we turn night into day with electrically simulated daylight in our homes and outside on the street. As a result, we never know what Real is. Is it any wonder that our hold on reality is tenuous at best?

Okay. So I wouldn't want to give up my electric furnace in wintertime or the tempering effect of air conditioning on summer heat. Most of the time, at least, I wouldn't want to throw out my clocks. And yet I've lived in places where I did without them—without telephones, central heat, even without electricity. I wouldn't want to do it again.

Let's face it. I'm attached to my wires—especially the ones that make heat not so hot and cold not so cold. But that doesn't mean that I've given up on pursuing life beyond the wires.

Maybe it's because of a lifelong effort to separate my grade-school fantasy from reality that I hold those rare moments of brain-singeing clarity as near-sacred. At times like these, when experience is incontestably Real and I have thrown off the Pinocchio strings that connect me with the master mechanism, I am real, too. Such an encounter erupts unexpectedly and short-circuits the whole wired apparatus.

These unexpected encounters come more often here where the sea has already unlatched the door to a capacity for wider experience. The sea with its awesome breadth and ever-changing motion sets us up. We're open to anything that happens. And so it was this very morning when we met the elephants of the sea.

The morning begins like any ordinary day in May at the tropical seashore. The smell of brewing coffee penetrates the salt sea air. People in swimsuits, towels slung around their shoulders, wander out onto the beach, still holding their cups and dazed with sleep. All of us are drawn to the ritual. We spill from our rooms to greet the morning and see what's going on out at sea.

None of us realizes that this particular day will change us, and even so, that the change will be brought on by something as unremarkable as a touch.

Already, looking out over the wide water, we can see that there's something out there. In the high surf, dark shapes nearly as big as automobiles are barely visible as they move slowly along just under the surface. Now and then a nose the size of a walrus snout pokes above the waves and quickly submerges again. What's going on out there?

A crowd from upbeach has gathered around these mysterious shapes and moves with them in the sea as they head south a dozen yards from shore. I slosh through the water to join the group. About fifteen people wade along, waist-deep, joggled by the ocean's surge. Dark shapes loom all around us. There are six, or maybe eight. And they are huge. No more than indistinct shadows under the water's surface, they—the things—graze the murky sea bottom almost out of sight. Like underwater lawn mowers, they nibble their way along. Now and then, they surface with a loud snort.

"What *are* they?" a woman next to me blurts, her blue baseball cap shading pixie sunglasses. Voices chime in. "They're manatees," one says. Another adds, "We call them sea cows." "Sea dogs," someone else offers. "I've heard they're elephants of the sea," says a blond-haired man with a sunburnt nose. Their name doesn't seem to matter. We follow them like curious children as they move along, nearly hidden, among us.

I remember reading about manatees, sometimes called sea elephants because, oddly enough, elephants are their closest relatives. Imagine, if you will, an elephant with its trunk—how shall we say—*truncated?* Its floppy Dumbo ears and hind legs missing. Its forelegs turned into flippers and its curly tail enlarged nearly to the size of a bulldozer shovel. You hold now in your mind's eye the image of a sea elephant, the gentle, friendly manatee.

Manatees, I've read, are shy, slow, docile. Adults may weigh up to half a ton or more and measure eight to ten feet, nose to tail. It's rare to spot them grazing in the open ocean. Usually they prefer to hang out along inland waterways.

What I remember most from reading about them is that elephants of the sea have been around for some forty million years. Yet their future is in question. While individual animals can live nearly as long as we do, forty-one percent of the number who perish before their time die as a result of injuries from motorboat propellers. The ones who survive are left with horrifyingly deep scars. Today, it's estimated there are only about eighteen hundred manatees still in existence worldwide.

Despite their plight, if you happen to catch a

glimpse of their faces, they appear to be smiling. They seem a cheerful lot. In fact, someone once told me these gentle, lumbering giants can whistle. I listen for the slightest hint of such a sound as a nose appears, here and there above the water, snorts a gush of spray, and submerges. No matter how hard I look, I still can't see them clearly. Their huge, heavy bodies grazing along the bottom have stirred up sand and debris that cloud the water.

Suddenly a massive form rises near the surface. I can see an animal's many-colored, furry hide break through the water. It reminds me of medieval writer Gottfried von Strassburg's description of a dog that Tristan gave to his ladylove, Isolde: "viewed against the grain, no one, no matter how clever, could possibly tell its hue; for it was often so many colors and all in such bewilderment, that it seemed to be none at all."

Right before my eyes, in this fleeting instant, the manatee's hide shows brown and red and black with patches of moss green—all "in such bewilderment." I am transfixed. Without my realizing it, my wires begin to loosen.

I ask a young woman who stands up to her chest in seawater next to me if she has touched one of the animals. We are moving along among them, our whole entourage heading slowly south. "Yes, they've allowed us to pet them—they even seem to like it," she says, wiping saltwater from her cheek. I ask what they feel like. "Sometimes a little slimy, sometimes furry."

A small plane puttering overhead, flying low, interrupts our conversation. Its underwing is inscribed with "Florida Sea Patrol" in letters large enough to see from the ground. The patrol is watching over the manatees, making sure no harm comes to them. Seconds later, a speedboat slices through the waves past our slowly progressing troupe of humans and manatees. The boat, too, is part of the patrol's surveillance of this endangered species.

The animals have moved ahead of us now as they graze their way along the sea bottom. They are moving into deeper water. It's hard to keep up with them, as we half-walk, half-swim in the heaving seawater. Manatees certainly have the edge over us frail, awkward humans.

I want to touch one. The woman's description isn't enough; I have to experience myself what it feels like. But I fear it's too late. The group of manatees has begun to move farther out, beyond our reach.

Just then, as if the animals can read my thoughts, the family of six or eight swings in again toward shore. This is my last chance. I swim hard, thrashing my arms in the water, to catch up with the dark shapes that creep like shadows beneath the swell. It's impossible to tell in the disturbed water exactly where they are. One moment we can see them surfacing, the next moment they disappear.

"Where *are* they?" I plead to a man at my elbow, his gray mustache beaded with saltwater and his battered straw hat pulled low over bushy brows.

"Right here!" he says. "Look!"

A broad gray nose pierces the water, snorts, and disappears. Its brown-black-red fur glistens when the animal moves past my leg, its body as broad as an overturned rowboat.

I stretch out a puny human hand, feeling around under the water like a blind person. And then! And then! I touch its fur. The manatee's heavy, solid, slippery, live, untamed body. It feels like the woman said: slimy and furry. In that instant's contact my foggy mind clears. The wires fall away. It's not so much that the world cracks open—but more like someone or something has quietly and conscientiously rearranged and fitted together the jumbled

pieces of a puzzle that in a flash of recognition has created a whole new picture, colorful and complete. I feel
not only the reality of the animal, but its mystery.

There's no mistaking that these gentle elephants
of the sea have taken a liking to us. Why? Is it because
they tolerate our presence? Or do they sense something in us, something that we rarely show—a playful, affectionate something that they respond to?
Certainly all they can see of us is our spindly legs and
flailing arms, weak by manatee measure. That certainly
couldn't have been what charmed them. Strict veg-
etarians, they wouldn't want to eat us even if they
could. So why? Why do they appear to like us?

Maybe the manatees' presumed affection for us
is what the Greek writer Plutarch calls "a friendship
for no advantage." They seem to like us—well—just
because. And we like them in the same way. Because
they're big. And odd. And friendly. We're not out
to capture them for Sea World or eat them for dinner.
Ours is, for once, "a friendship for no advantage."
What could we accomplish if we practiced such a thing
in everyday life, even among ourselves?

The animals move farther south in the shallow
water a few yards out from shore. And we let them
go. I wade ashore, examining my wet right hand as

if it has been tattooed with the image of the animal it touched. An elephant of the sea and I had made real contact. We reached out for each other and we touched. This contact with a creature whose hide feels like a slimy scrub brush has short-circuited the console. Pinocchio has come to life.

Want to Adopt a Manatee?

You can join the Save the Manatee Club's Adopt-a-Manatee-Program. They won't give you one to take home as a pet, but you can find out about your manatee as it lives in the wild through photos and information the club sends you. Your contribution supports programs that work to protect endangered manatees and their habitat.

Contact Save the Manatee Club, 500 N. Maitland Avenue, Maitland, FL 32751, 1-800-432-JOIN, or *www.savethemanatee.org*.

5

A Bouquet of Gull Feathers
Finding Something Sacred
in the Ordinary

But if you cultivate a healthy poverty and simplicity,
so that finding a penny will literally make your day,
then, since the world is in fact planted with pennies,
you have with your poverty bought a lifetime of days.
—ANNIE DILLARD, *Pilgrim at Tinker Creek*

 How do we know what is sacred? Whose job is it to tell us? Here at the seabeach where the wide horizon opens a trapdoor to the cellar parts of our minds, we begin to wonder about such things. We begin, as Alexandra Johnson says in *Leaving a Trace*, to "play detective to our own days . . . to uncover the extraordinary in the ordinary in daily life."

We could do this at home if we wanted to. If we took the time. If no other need pulled us away. But it's easier here, away from daily routines and demands. In the lull we can mull the deeper questions. The sea inspires such wonderings. Sometimes, as it did this morning, it even suggests a few answers.

As the sun, newly risen, struggles to warm the wind, I walk down the beach before breakfast. A stormy night sea has gouged away the sand, leaving jutting wedges that look like rows of stony sphinxes or ships' prows. Sand near the water's edge is polished smooth except for a few bleached shells.

Here an old woman stoops to retrieve something. Her black pucker-knit tube top stretches to accommodate ample breasts and bulges at the waist where it meets wide-cut shorts, flowered as wildly as a Georgia O'Keeffe painting. Her bare feet plod along in oversized athletic shoes. As she leans over, a few gray hairs escape the knot at her neck and fall in wisps over her sunglasses.

I ask what she's finding, pointing to the plastic bag she clutches in her hand. "Oh, just a few shells. Ordinary, really. The good ones have long since been picked up by others." She fingers a circle of gold beads, apparently real, around her neck—the

kind you buy one at a time at a jewelry store to com-
memorate a birthday or anniversary. "But I don't
look for shells," she continues. "I come here to find
feathers, and I've already found one this morning!"
She holds up a small gray gull feather still wet with
seawater. No doubt it had looked better on the gull.

"I've made a bouquet of them—these feathers—
and I add to it each time I find another one." She
looks at me from behind a wrinkled smile. "I guess
that sounds goofy, collecting gull feathers for a bouquet, but it's really pretty. You should see it."

I murmur that it's probably beautiful, although
looking at the ragged gray feather in her hand, I'm
having a hard time visualizing it. In my mind I'm
trying to picture a whole bouquet of these things—
feathers that have been stepped on by beach walkers,
tossed in and out by the waves, and adhered to by
sand and shell fragments like nuts on a taffy apple.
It's not a pretty picture.

We walk on in opposite directions as I continue
to struggle with the image of a gull feather bouquet,
gray and weathered as driftwood. I remember something Sue Bender said in *Everyday Sacred:* "Maybe the
most sacred things are the hardest to see, because
they are so obvious." Do we overlook the sacred,

planted as profusely as pennies in our world, because such things are right in front of us? Maybe so.

We grow immune to things we see every day. The everyday world bores us. I remember an article I once read in the _New York Times_ by James Traub, an American who described an outdoor dinner he attended in Aurangabad, India. During the meal he sat beside an Indian man and the two became engaged in conversation, the tropical night forming a dark, star-scattered ceiling high above them. Midway into the conversation, the Indian man gestured toward the stars and said in all seriousness, "Do you enjoy the sky where you live?"

Do we? Do we enjoy the sky where we live? The ordinary sky we see every cloudless night? Is this even a question we'd ask a dinner partner in our own town under our own patch of sky? Most of us don't realize that common things like stars and feathers and pennies have their own importance. They may even have something to tell us.

I often ask students in my writing and journaling classes to bring in an object they're attached to— something that has no value except to them. They bring the most incredible things.

Once a young woman who was married with two

small children brought her bridal bouquet to class. "I never save anything," she said, "but I just couldn't throw this away." The flowers in the bouquet hadn't been preserved by any means other than natural drying, which left them looking even more forlorn than this morning's wet and salty gull feathers the Feather Lady had proudly shown me. But somehow the bride bouquet with the fading blue streamers and the brown dead flowers had meant something to the woman in my class. The bouquet was a sacred, if pitiful, object.

Other objects that people have brought to class are just as odd, yet just as ordinary. There was a coffee mug, a dark green ceramic souvenir of the Smoky Mountains, whose owner proclaimed, "I can't drink coffee in the morning if I don't have my mug. If it's in the dishwasher and hasn't been washed, I haul it out and wash it." These ordinary objects possess the power of attachment that can't always be explained. People have brought to class such things as an absent father's bronze wrestling medal, a clay bowl made by a son at summer camp, and a red plastic Chinese chest. None of these would bring much at a swap meet. Yet to someone, at least, they were important—perhaps everyday sacred.

Sometimes you don't know the value of something until you've lost it. A man who is staying with his wife in the rooms above mine here at the beach, tells me he lost a coin purse he left at Barnes and Noble this morning. The thing is of no special value, he says. It was a freebee from a hotel in Daytona Beach, where he had stayed on a business trip years ago. The purse held just small change, less than a dollar. "But I've grown attached to it over the years. For some strange reason it has tremendous emotional value," he said. So he called the bookstore. They had found the change purse, and he drove back to fetch it. He was happy as a kid finding a new penny.

Why do we value certain things of little value to other people, things that might be overlooked at a garage sale? Maybe it's because these objects are bigger than they look. They hold our hopes, our dreams, our sense of self, our connectedness to other people and to the world. We don't always recognize their significance in the beginning.

I once owned a Virgin Islands air plant I called Tommy, which flourished for years in my windowsill at home. It began as a succulent leaf I brought back from the islands in my suitcase. Within a few weeks, the leaf, sustained by nothing but air, had sprouted tiny new plants along its edges. When the plants were transplanted into their own pots where they thrived on sun and moisture, they soon grew so big that they constantly had to be cut back and repotted.

Not being much of a gardener, I got rid of all but one plant eventually, and gave only casual attention to the sole survivor. This lone plant was wily and resourceful. It could grow from any part of itself: root, stem, or leaf. It reminded me of myself at the time and how I'd come through difficulty using, mostly, devious wiles of adaptation. As time went on, I took for granted that the thing would live on despite my benign neglect. When I'd go on a trip, I'd chop off the plant at its root and plunk the cutting into a glass of water. When I came back, the plant had rerooted and sucked up the water to preserve its life.

But one winter when I was submerged in writing, I often let the plant go dry. I hadn't bothered to repot it after the last trip, so there was no earth to sustain it. There came a time when it was too late to add water. The plant was failing. It had used up every drop except what clung to its slimy roots. Only one leaf remained, as tiny as a child's fingernail, much smaller than the original one from which it had sprung. Ultimately, even that leaf moldered and died. I was overcome with regret.

When had I become attached to this green, unattractive thing whose only good quality was that it could obstinately reproduce itself despite shameful neglect? How does such attachment begin? St. Exupery in *The Little Prince* says it's through our daily care for some live thing. He cites as case in point the finicky rose that the Little Prince cared for; he watered her, talked to her, sheltered her from the wind. But I had done little for my poor neglected air plant, and despite myself, or it, had grown attached without even realizing it. Maybe it was, as the man said about his coin purse, that the thing had shared my life for so long.

Still, that theory doesn't explain the Feather Lady's passion for gull feathers. Somehow she has imposed sacredness on the gray feathers she finds. How does this happen?

These questions swim in my mind as I reach my usual turnaround point on my beach walk: a chickee hut, its weathered thatch roof strung with sun-bleached queen conchs that hang like a bulbous bead curtain around its edges. The chickee marks the halfway point between the place I'm staying and Doc's, a public hangout that serves breakfast and beer and, on weekends, packs the beach for a half mile in either direction. Like a trolley on a rail, I turn around to head back.

Still mulling how sacredness happens, I remember a woman I once knew who collected African artifacts. She lived in a vast barn of a place that had once been a dance studio. In the central high-ceilinged dance-studio-turned-living-room, she displayed a dozen dark wood African ceremonial figures, towering taller than their owner. The figures with their vaguely human features surrounded the sitting area of the living room with their imposing presence.

A group of us once had a meeting in that room. Encircled almost to suffocation by the leering, fierce-faced figures, we tried to concentrate on the business at hand. We couldn't. "We'll have to go to another room," the hostess said. "But don't feel bad—even my husband and I can hardly stand to be in here."

The memory of these bigger-than-life figures stuck with me. They were made of wood, probably a log from a tall tree. Nothing spooky in that. Carved and painted, the figures had been used in African religious rituals that none of us understood or even knew about. So how are these powers communicated?

I wondered if something held sacred endowed it with a special energy, an energy that even people who don't share the sense of sacredness can feel.

The natives of Peru seem to have a handle on this question, though they might be reluctant or unable to express their reasonings. They call anything they see that they think has some supernatural quality *"huaca."* Helpful spirits, they believe, are all around them and participate in their daily lives in subtle ways. The natives believe *huacas* possess special powers and can be anything from an oddly shaped rock to a body of water. Ordinary things become extraordinary to them, sometimes even sacred.

I'm a skeptic. I'd like to say it's all in people's minds, just like beauty is in the mind of the Feather Lady. But then, isn't everything we know, think, feel, intuit, in our minds? Skeptic or not, it's hard to ignore what happens when something—anything—is considered with passion as wonderful in its own right. It's possible to start with any object. A penny. A cup. Even a feather. We can imbue such things with sacredness until they radiate reflections of our passion. Once we're able to see objects as they really are, in the fullness of their being, could we not also apply our sense of sacredness to other human beings? To our

world at large? Who knows. We might create an out-
break of peacefulness!

Objects, of course, are easier to start with. They
rarely disappoint or talk back. I wonder if the Feather
Lady could be on to something. Today a feather,
tomorrow the world.

I think about her as a gull flies low, careening
above my head, screeching its rusty-gate cry. And
then I see her again. She stands flatfootedly in her
big athletic shoes in the sand farther down the beach.
The Feather Lady. Both arms wave enthusiastically
as if she's swimming in air. There's something in
her right hand. Coming closer, I can see it's a gull
feather.

"Look! I found another one! *Two* in one day!
Usually I find only one, even after I've been all up
and down the beach," she exclaims breathlessly,
poking a feather under my nose. "It's a gift, like Anne
Lindbergh says in her *Gift from the Sea.* Only this—this
is a gift from the *sky!*"

She pauses, looking at the feather, damp in her
hand, then blurts: "Am I crazy or what?"

"No," I say. "I think you're saner than most of
us." Like Annie Dillard's pennies, she has with her
gull feathers bought "a lifetime of days."

6

Invasion of the Red Tide
Death as Prelude

Transformation always occurs through a renuncia-
tion, a loss, a destruction.
> —ALDO CAROTENUTO, *The Vertical Labyrinth*

The sea has its wily ways. As life-giving wet nurse it nurtures a phantasmagoria of wildlife: anemones, sponges, jellyfish, coral, sea fans, fishes, shelled creatures. But it can also be a death-dealing destroyer. We're not usually aware of this destructive capacity until a lifeless something washes ashore.

This morning hundreds—no thousands—of lifeless somethings have washed up on the beach. Once, these somethings were fish. Now it's hard to tell, from their varying states of decomposition, just what they are. The only way you're sure these gelatinous gray things are fish is by their smell. They don't just smell bad—they fill your nostrils with stink, they saturate your clothes with stink, they invade your hair with stink. The beach is littered with death and its all-pervasive smell.

The sea is responsible. It has turned orange-brown with what I discover is called the red tide. Made up of millions of microscopic organisms poisonous to sea life, the scourge stretches for miles up and down the seacoast.

The red tide organisms put out a scent half way between sharp pine needles and hot red pepper that burns inside your nose and throat and causes convulsive coughing. Dinoflagellates—that's what the organisms are called—are normally present in seawater, but rarely in the overpowering numbers that cause the red tide. Certain conditions, including pollution, conspire to create the unexpected havoc lethal to fish and other sea creatures.

While the stench released by this widespread death and decay is tolerable in the early morning, by noon it becomes unbearable. Throat constricts. Nostrils burn. The smell is overwhelming. As dead fish cook in the hot sun, fishy odors begin to invade even sealed off rooms along the beach. By noon almost everyone has left the beach to seek refuge on the bay side of the island.

In hopes of finding relief, I drive north to the tip of the island, then down the other side. The air is better here. I walk out the long City Pier that protrudes several blocks into the bay like a giant tongue depressor. Here and there along its length, fishermen stand near the edge with their lines in the water. At the end of the pier, a restaurant forms a "T."

Inside the air-cooled dining room, tall windows offer an unobstructed view of the bay, where a mile or so across the water the Sunshine Skyway Bridge arches a hundred feet above the water to span the 4.1 miles across Tampa Bay. From here, the bridge looks like a mirage. Rising from mist and glinting golden in the sun, it could be a gilded rainbow.

Yet even on this protected side of the island, I can see near shore a few bloated pearly-gray fish bodies floating in the quiet water. I avert my eyes and try to concentrate on the menu. A waitress in white shorts and turquoise T-shirt breezes up to my table, pencil in hand and smiling. I order something called "seared tuna strips" with asparagus and red potatoes, and she sashays away toward the kitchen.

It's hard to think about food with my clothes still

reeking of dead fish. Against my will, I begin instead to think of death. How often does such a thought intrude? Seldom. By trying not to think about death, I hope to keep it stashed in some far corner of my mind. I am trying to do that now. Walled in by glass that separates me from the gray bodies in the bay, I try to focus on the golden arches of the bay bridge. The distraction isn't working. People at other tables all around me are coughing and blowing their noses, even though the air is better here. Their coughing and blowing reminds me of what I don't want to be reminded of.

So I concentrate on the catsup bottle in the middle of the varnished pine table where I sit. A fly explores the sweet red ooze under its cap, and I think, without wanting to, about beginnings and endings. Mostly about endings.

A few years ago when I was teaching a writing class for cancer patients, I was shocked, appalled even, when one woman in the class said that cancer was the best thing that ever happened to her. She wore a scarf tied around her head to cover the effects of chemo; her pale cheeks were sunken and gaunt. *How could cancer be a good thing? People* die *of cancer.* My incredulous look must have betrayed me. The woman explained:

"It's only with the threat of death that I learned how to live." A small spark made its way into her hollow eyes when she spoke. "It's only then—only with that threat—that you begin to realize what's really important in life. The greatest tragedy is to be dead before you die." A smile broke out on the pale tallow of her face as her thin lips spread in an expression of agonized happiness.

She left the class early that day, handing me a note as she went out. "I loved the class," the note read, "but I'm feeling very tired and need to go home to rest." Two days later she died.

I swallow hard, remembering, as the waitress brings my meal. The tuna arrives encrusted with sesame seeds. Beside it sits a pink rose made of marinated ginger curls. The rose reminds me of the woman in the scarf whose name, I grieve to say, I can't remember. The tuna tastes good. It smells like tuna ought to. Appetizing. The meal restores my morale. Afterward, I take a notebook and pen I've brought with me and what's left of a beer I ordered to a table outside.

It's almost too hot to write out here. But there's a breath of a breeze that makes the pier underneath my chair sway just enough to create a slight disequilibrium. Strange that they'd have a restaurant way out here, clear at the end of a long stretch of wooden pier. Once, they say, in the midst of a hurricane, the whole place left its moorings and took off into the water. Whoosh. Just like that it was gone.

It took a long time to rebuild. But now the diners are back. So are the fishermen who sit on their knot-holed gray wood benches, casting, casting for some elusive fish they likely would not eat even if one swallowed the bait. It's a wonder, in any case, that live fish still swim in the red water that has belched so many corpses. Blessedly, red tide is rare, and on the bay side, not even red.

Thinking about death has made me remember difficult endings. When my mother died suddenly following my father's death several years before, a friend and coworker who had also lost both parents said to me, "now we are orphans." What a curious thing to say. I'd always pictured orphans as young and poor, like Oliver Twist. But there I was, an adult orphan. Not poor, but alone, with no one to blame or credit with my successes and failures. It's an enormous responsibility, being an orphan.

We are all orphans, in one way or another, alone inside ourselves. Solitude is good practice for us. It opens us to the realization of who we are—who we *really* are. Solitude is an opportunity to stand apart, a spirit quest, an initiation. You can take it or leave it as you will. There is, in any case, a price to pay if the call goes unheeded.

"The need for some kind of initiation is so important that if it does not happen consciously, it will happen unconsciously, often in a dangerous form," I read in *Betwixt and Between,* edited by Louise Carus Mahdi, Steven Foster, and Meredith Little. People in primitive tribes knew this. That's why their initiations into adulthood were often so intentionally horrific they created in the young initiates the sense of impending death. As the woman with cancer said, it is only in facing the threat of death that anyone can "really know how to live."

Solitude, being alone with oneself, can be an initiation, because it strips away all the usual supports and false faces. The public self goes. The Real Self begins to incubate and take form. Somewhere in the process a part of you dies and another part of you comes into exuberant life.

"Would you like another beer?" the waitress, who has found me even at my outside table, asks. I nod. She's off to fetch another. The familiarly pleasant smell of fried burgers couples with the piquant scent of fishsauce out here among the tables where diners feed like sharks from paper-lined baskets heaped with fries. I can't see them unless I turn around, but I can hear the drone of their voices and the scrape of their metal chairlegs on the deck.

A breeze picks up. It blows pleasantly cool across the bay and wrinkles the water into waves of shallow confusion near shore. Farther out, small storms float by like colossal jellyfish, tendrils of rain streaming from their puffy shapes. The wind shifts to the west and takes most of the fishy smell with it. Yet, now and then, all around me, people are still coughing from their exposure on the other side.

Fishermen on their benches a few feet away haven't been getting much action. Are there any live fish left in the bay? I wonder how long fish live and whether they've had a fulfilling life before some of them met their end from the red tide. Do they even know what a fulfilling life is? Or, more importantly, do we? Death may be the great motivator. If death doesn't raise its head at least once in a while during a life, we could put off real living forever. But hints of mortality remind us, when death comes up and spits in our eye and says, "folks, this is all there is. Make the most of it."

So we gallop off in the opposite direction, full speed. Juggle a million things at once. Rush. Never enough time. Hurry. We haven't got forever. We end up driving on empty, never realizing the tank needs desperately to be refilled.

That happened to me after my last book, *Pencil Dancing,* was finally finished. I'd put blood, sweat, tears, outrageous joy, and every scrap of everything I knew into those pages. When the last word was written, and I'd shipped the manuscript off to the publisher, I had expected to be overflowing with exhilaration. I wasn't. Just the opposite. I felt emptied, unmotivated, confused, and consumed by a creative black hole. What I experienced was writer's postpartum depression, and it made me feel like my last child had just left home. It felt a lot like a death, even though, eventually, it was a creative rebirth.

But I hadn't a clue how to renew at the time. Shouldn't I be full of vigor and ready to jump into another book? What's wrong here? I had no one to ask. Samuel Clemens (Mark Twain) might have diagnosed my difficulties as death by overemptying. But he would have had a solution. He once said that when the tank runs dry you only have to leave it a while and it will fill up again.

No one can exist without replenishing. Take cows, for example. They have to nibble the lush prairie grasses all day long in order to produce just one tin pail of milk. In this way, we're no different from cows. Whether we're parents or teachers or executives or construction workers or garbage collectors or writers, we each need to refill ourselves when we're emptied out. We can't depend on other people to fill us. We have to learn to feed ourselves and we have to know *when*. Like the tides, life runs in highs and lows. The challenge is to know how to surf each one.

A cold beer miraculously appears in front of me. The waitress must have come and gone without my noticing, I am so deep into thinking about death. As I sip the bitter-tasting bubbles, I remember a morning on the beach a few days earlier when I found something I'd never seen before.

At first, I didn't know what the thing was. The irregularly shaped rectangle, about the size of a snack cracker, felt light and delicate as an eggshell in my palm. On one side it looked varnished, the shine shading to ochre at the edges with a large "V" incised in the center. The reverse side was etched with a raised pattern of branching ridges that resembled a tree to which dried yolk-like shreds still clung.

"What is this?" I asked a woman walking by who held several seashells in her hands. "It's a crab belly," she said. "Or was." She explained how the crab would have worn this armor, shiny side out, as protection for its tender insides. What happened to the rest of him? Was he eaten by a seabird, his pinchers, legs, and upper shell drifting their separate ways in the surf? Was his death painful? Can crabs feel? I wondered whether he'd be reincarnated as a crab or come back in another life as a cow or an alligator or even a human. Or come back at all.

I continue to ponder the crab's demise as I watch beads of moisture trickle down the beer glass in front of me. Perhaps my own time will come as unexpectedly as the crab's. It seems, if we're open to it, there are many opportunities to practice dying even as we continue fully to live. Every major—or even minor—change is preceded by the death of whatever came before. A natural cycle: beginning, middle, end. And then another beginning.

Warm air and the beer are beginning to make me sleepy. I pack up my pen and notebook and head back down the pier toward shore. Surely by now, with the sun slowly sinking toward the horizon, the rotting fish smell will have abated back at the beach.

True, the air here on the beach side does seem better. I decide to go for a walk to clear my head from the beer, and as a precaution, grab a washcloth to take along to cover my face in case the stench is bad. Certainly the odor won't be quite so strong in the cooler air of evening, and I don't want to miss the nightly ritual of sunset-watching.

But out on the beach, as the light fades and the breeze increases, there are thousands, maybe hundreds of thousands of dead fish washed up on shore, rotting. Covering my face with the washcloth from my room, I try to step among them. Sometimes I miss. The sickening squish of decaying fish underfoot is not a sensation to be savored. One fish I step on gives up its guts and spurts onto my shoe—new white sneakers I'd bought at K-Mart just a few days before.

I go back to my room to try to wash off the awful stuff in the bathroom sink, only to discover that the stepped-upon fish had adhered to the sole of my shoe as well. When I've cleaned up as much as I can, the whole place smells of rotten fish. I feel frustrated knowing that tomorrow will likely be worse.

It's a relief when someone tells me that the city will send cleanup crews in the morning to cart away the tons of dead fish washed up on the sand. This good news, the meal at City Pier—or maybe the beer—lift my spirits. I imagine that along the shore there flies a seabird nourished by the dead crab whose shell I held in my hand days before, and by the feast of dead fishes on the beach. A vision lingers that death supports life. Endings spawn beginnings. The sea participates in the circle of life and death, favoring neither one nor the other. Life goes on.

7

The Storm Before the Calm
Riding Out a Hurricane Alone

*Though emotional storms may uproot us, weaken
our bodies and personalities, they may just as well
serve to deepen us—to make us more vivid, more
intensely us.*

—STANLEY KELEMAN, *Your Body Speaks Its Mind*

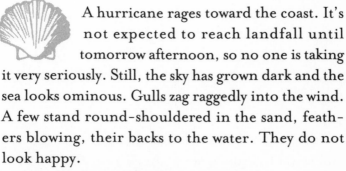 A hurricane rages toward the coast. It's
not expected to reach landfall until
tomorrow afternoon, so no one is taking
it very seriously. Still, the sky has grown dark and the
sea looks ominous. Gulls zag raggedly into the wind.
A few stand round-shouldered in the sand, feathers blowing, their backs to the water. They do not
look happy.

Rain has been falling heavily all afternoon. But
now it lets up long enough for me to make a dash to

refill my rental car's tank in case there's an evacuation. Already, deep puddles of rain flood the narrow beach road. With no gutters to run down, no drains— only sand to soak up the water as best it can—the downpour has no place to go. There is little traffic, in any case, and I drive around the puddles with ease.

The storm subsides for a moment while I gas up and stop at Mr. Bones for carryout on my way back. At least a good meal will sustain me if I have to leave in the morning to drive farther inland. In the sack with the rice, cole slaw, and apricot chicken, I stow a bottle of Heineken, to make a hurricane party for one.

When I return to my place, the office calls to suggest a move to the back of the complex, farthest from the water. I repack and drag my suitcase and the supper from Mr. Bones to the new room, leaving the rest of the food behind until morning when I plan to retrieve it before the storm hits. Little do I know that this will be my last real meal for several days.

It's dark by the time I unpack the apricot chicken and settle into my new room. Already the wind has picked up and stirs the palms outside my window into an agitated dance. As I finish the last of the chicken and sip the Heineken straight from the bottle, a TV weathercaster announces "voluntary evacuation" of the island. The announcement seems redundant. There is almost no one left to evacuate except me and a few others. The staff has gone for the night and won't be back in the morning. Anyone planning to arrive has canceled. Everyone else, except for one couple a few doors away, has left.

I'm not due to leave for another week, and besides, I have nowhere to go. Now, in the dark, I wouldn't know how to get there if I did. Like it or not, I have no choice but to ride out the storm alone. At midnight, with the hurricane reportedly at least ten or twelve hours away, I switch off the TV and go to sleep.

At 6:00 A.M., howling wind wakes me. I've never heard anything like it, except once in a while during a blizzard in the far north. It's still completely dark outside and impossible to tell how much the sea is rising. A click onto the TV news verifies what I can already hear outside: the storm is escalating into a stage-one hurricane. Wind and rain lash against the door so hard it won't open. It's like being sealed in an automobile while thrashing through a car wash. The only sound is the rage of water.

TV announcers advise everyone still on the island

to stay inside, off the roads that are already flooded from the blowing rain. Every once in a while the TV goes off for a second or two along with the lights. Broadcasters caution that what they're calling "a borderline hurricane" sits off shore and gathers strength minute by minute.

At 6:15 A.M., suddenly the lights go out and the TV picture dissolves. Everything goes black. The room is as dark as the inside of a coal mine. No shapes stand out. Nothing. No news from the mute TV whether we should evacuate or stay, worry or not worry. Me, I'm worried.

Though nothing can be seen in the dark, the storm still can be heard. It moans and raps on the roof, rushes against the window, roars through the palm branches. How long until the light comes? An hour? Two? In the dark I fall into fitful sleep.

It's almost nine when I wake. Cold, raw wind and rain pour through a gap in the sliding glass window. In my nightgown, I get up to stuff the crack with wadded Kleenex. That works pretty well. The electricity is still out and the front door held shut by a deluge of water blown against it. My food, sorry to say, is down the open hall, out of reach until the storm subsides. To make matters worse, all the leftover chicken from Mr. Bones will likely have spoiled by now. These small refrigerators struggle even under best conditions and certainly won't keep food cold very long without power.

Still no word on the weather. I'm forced to do my own prediction, as people once did before forecasters helped out, by looking out the window. Even then, it's impossible to tell what's happening. One moment there's a lull, a few seconds later an avalanche of water hurls down in all directions. The window rattles. Palms bend nearly to the ground. Is it getting worse or better? It's impossible to tell.

How long do these storms last? The announcer had advised at 6:00 A.M., much too late for me to comply, that one should have a week's supply of provisions, a battery radio, and a flashlight. All I have is a flashlight, its batteries already going dim. At least I had the foresight to bring along a bag of oat bran from the other room. Oat bran is breakfast this morning. It will likely be lunch, too, the way things look with the rain raging outside like a whirlwind, showing no sign of letup.

Doubtless I'll have to make a run for it at some point to rescue what little food is still safe to eat in the other room closer to the beach. What will be left? I suppose I could subsist on sesame blue corn chips, oat bran, Wasa flatbread, and water for a few days if I have to.

This is going to be a long, long day. No TV. No phone. Little food. There's nothing to do but watch the storm and write. What do people do who are marooned on an island or imprisoned in a cell? I have new empathy for them. Like an Inuit trapped in an igloo all winter, I take up a craft to pass the time. I write. At least, with the window chinked with tissue, I am warm and dry. So far, so good. A sense of almost-relief spreads over me. For the moment, I feel self-reliant and brave.

In the past hour, the storm seems to be getting worse. Rain doesn't simply fall, or even blow, but combats itself, blows back into its own force, then reverses as if it can't make up its mind where to direct its frenzy. So much rain is falling that it obscures the building next door, only twenty or thirty feet away. This must be what it feels like to be a plate inside a dishwasher, water rushing madly in all directions. On my way to the bathroom, I pass the front door. Rain has poured in underneath and my socks squish on the wet carpet.

I do a noontime weather check using the only tool

I have: a look out the window. It's hard to see what's happening out to sea, but when the wind blows some of the palm branches aside, it's suddenly clear that the water has enveloped the beach and moved all the way up to the border of sea oats. There's no beach at all, any more. To get a look landward, I squish to the door. I wait till I hear the wind die down a little, then push open the door to a blast of rain in my face. In the instant before the door blows shut, I can see there's now only one other car in the lot besides mine. The thought is comforting that at least I'm not completely alone.

Although the storm still rages, the sky appears to be brightening. Maybe that's just because it's noon. What do I know about these things? Outside, the ground is littered with palm fronds, sea grape leaves, and pathetically rain-squashed hibiscus flowers. One of the light globes near the pool has been blown off its post and has broken into shards on the grass. Still the rain thunders down.

It's well past lunchtime, and even though I'm not hungry, there's an empty gnaw in my stomach. The storm has been raging since last night, and all I've had to eat all day is a few spoonfuls of oat bran. Should I run the gauntlet out on the open passageway to try to get to the other room and what's left of the food? Will the storm lessen soon so the overhang will offer some protection, unlike now with the rain gusting sideways? I decide to chance it.

I force open the door and run headlong down the open corridor, fending off a gush of wind and water, poke the key in the hole, and burst into my old room. It seems like a familiar friend, quiet, unscathed by the storm. All the packages of food are still where I left them. I grab what I can, chuck everything into plastic grocery store bags, and race back down the windy passageway to what I now think of as "the safe room."

Lunch is sesame blue corn chips and what's left of a quart of fresh grapefruit juice that I'm trusting is still good after half a day in a nonfunctioning refrigerator. With nothing else to do after a spartan lunch, I nap for half an hour. When I wake, the sky is clearer, almost sunny, even though, perversely, the rain continues to fall and wind is strong as ever. The storm seems about to abate. I figure I'll wait an hour and try to get out to find some fresh flashlight batteries and a candle or two. Electricity is still out.

I throw open the door and make a dash for the car. When I turn the corner of the building, wind heaves me back and flings sand and debris into my face. I can't see. Back to the room. Open and close the door with all my strength. Rats! The storm has suddenly stirred again. It hurls bucketfuls of rain at anything in its way. The water is so thick it looks like those gel window sprays, the drops huge and blobby and fiercely flung. In less than four hours it will be dark again, and all I have for light is a dying flashlight.

I'm trapped. This is not solitude, this is imprisonment! Oh, what I'd give for just a half hour of TV or even one person to talk to. Such contact would relieve the feeling that I'm a kite that's lost its tether, flying aimlessly in space.

How do people cope with solitary confinement? I think about prisoners locked away in cells for years and years, alone, nothing to occupy their minds. What do they do? You can only sleep just so long. You can only write just so long. But I dare not stop. Writing is a way to keep functioning, to stay at least minimally sane.

Like most people, I've always sought solitude, but the kind I wanted was *voluntary.* The kind where you could take a break when you wanted to, go in and out of it like the tide. This storm-imposed solitude is mandatory. No choice. You're here for the duration and you don't know how long that will be. From the looks of the bluster outside, too long.

It would be different if I weren't alone. If there were someone to talk to, to check things out with, to be brave for, I might not need a writing marathon.

At five o'clock, anticipating a long dark night without electricity, I decide to try again to get batteries and candles. The open hall is like a wind tunnel and a forceful gust drives me back on the first try, my eyes smarting from blown sand and saltwater. So I pull a plastic bag over my head, holding it out at the bottom just enough to breathe and force my way against the wind down the corridor and stairway to the car. Once inside and protected from wind and rain, the drive isn't as bad as I'd anticipated. The road is even more flooded than before and I have to drive slowly through the deep water. Stop lights are out, but with only a few cars on the road, it isn't a problem.

With the power out, many businesses are closed. So I'm relieved when I get to the drug store, and a young man opens the door for me. They allow in only three people at a time, he says, because the lights aren't working. Inside, except for light through the front windows, the store remains dark. With the aid of a flashlight, the young man accompanies me from one department to another. They've sold out of radios, but have one radio/tape player left. I take it. On to the candles, then batteries. At the checkout, the clerk tallies the sale by hand as two tiny battery-operated plastic fans provide some cool. The young man has to push open what had been an automatic door when I leave. I'm nearly swept away by wind outside, but once inside the car, the return trip is easy.

Back in my "safe" room, I listen anxiously to the weather report on my new $12.95 radio stereo cassette player. The storm, forecasters say, is largely over. Despite its seventy to eighty MPH wind gusts, it doesn't quite make it to official hurricane strength, falling short by only one MPH.

As night closes in, I light three votive candles—good for eight hours—and sit down at the dining table to enjoy a sumptuous meal of corn thinbread, almond butter, and an apple salvaged from the other room. Candlelight is calming after all the confusion of the past three days. The room huddles in silence with no sound but the tick of the battery-run wall clock and the wash of waves. There's a storm advisory until midnight, but already the wind has stopped rattling windows and has given up its howl. Most of the storm has moved on to Orlando, where it rages down upon Mickey, Goofy, and the Disney gang. Before bed, I blow out the candles and the room goes dark.

In the middle of the night I'm startled awake as the electric lights suddenly snap on. Glory be! Power surges once again. Phones work (I checked). The TV functions (I checked that, too). And lamps cast an orienting light that defines the room and tells me where I am. I turn off the lights and go back to sleep, dreaming of a magical child with golden hair who gives me an arrangement of purple roses, jewels, and seashells.

At eight o'clock the day begins in sunshine and blue sky. A few people straggle out onto the beach like ants from a drowned anthill. The storm has moved on and brought fresh, cool, air from the north. Newscasters say that yesterday's rain measured nearly nine inches in a few hours—an all-time record.

The weathermaker seems to beg forgiveness this morning. A more perfect day is beyond imagination: calm seas, cool breeze, and blue sky vaulting, cloudless, from one edge of the horizon to the other.

A quiet sea rolls in neatly, its border crocheted with white lace foam. Gulls fill the sky, circling like torn paper in a wind tunnel, diving and rising. The air is a-tingle with their shrieks and cries.

After the storm, as naturally as day follows night, comes the lull, the peace, the sense of having made it through. After all, isn't that the way life works: first the trial, then the reward? How else, except by stark contrast, could we recognize our blessings when they show up? So, in a way, a storm is a blessing, too. It brings the ecstasy of afterward when you've endured the fury of the whirlwind and the long, dark night alone.

8

Seacatchers
"A Gift *for* the Sea"

If the only prayer you say in your entire life is thank you, that would be enough.

—MEISTER ECKHARDT

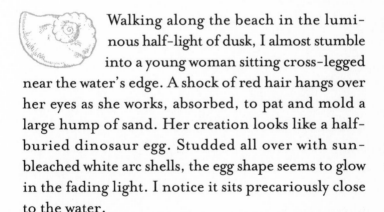 Walking along the beach in the luminous half-light of dusk, I almost stumble into a young woman sitting cross-legged near the water's edge. A shock of red hair hangs over her eyes as she works, absorbed, to pat and mold a large hump of sand. Her creation looks like a half-buried dinosaur egg. Studded all over with sun-bleached white arc shells, the egg shape seems to glow in the fading light. I notice it sits precariously close to the water.

"You're an optimist," I say, pointing to the incoming tide, drawing closer and about to devour her shell-jeweled egg.

"Oh no, not at all!" she says, looking up, her white smile wide in the near dark. "I know the sea will take it and it will be gone in the morning. That's why I made it. It's a *gift for the sea,* a kind of 'thank you.'"

Imagine. A thank-you gift for the sea. What a wonderfully quirky idea. To carve out a moment for gratitude and to express that feeling by building a gift of sand. Could that be what inspires the making of these sand sculptures, what I call seacatchers, that wait for the water to enter and claim them?

Such imaginative constructions keep appearing up and down the beach. Every day there are at least one or two. Some are as intricate as catacombs, with tiny, neatly molded stairs that ascend and descend. Some are elaborate castles surrounded by walls and moats. Still others are simple like this one. All are seacatchers. They lie close to the water's edge, ready to sacrifice themselves to the next high tide. Most have a channel leading inward to welcome the sea when it comes.

For a long time I puzzled over why ordinary people who have never before built a moat or turret or

mound or sand wall suddenly turn into sculptors at
the beach. What inspires them? Why do they, in the
presence of sand and water, suddenly turn into beach
artists? It's a mystery.

It's easy to understand why someone might try to
make a device to capture some seawater to take home.
But these seacatchers are made as an offering, a sacrifice to the sea. The sea enters, consumes the sand
structure, and returns to its bed, gratified.

Seacatchers appear in as many forms as there are
imaginations to make them. A few days ago, walking
along the beach with my cap pulled down to shield
my face from the late afternoon sun, I nearly fell
into a bathtub-shaped excavation in the sand.
Someone had dug a hollow, built up its rim,
smoothed the bottom and sides with care. The tub had
withstood the night tides and still lay intact only a
few yards from the water.

Why would someone build such a thing? I imagine a tyke, or even a grownup, stretched out in the
completed sand tub with only a head sticking up.
Passers-by would be startled to see a disembodied
head lying on the sand, perhaps getting ready to roll
like a beach ball into the water. The person whose
head stuck out from the hole might feel like a newly

hatched turtle struggling to emerge from its nest, seeing the light of day for the first time.

But the person who created the sand tub is long gone. I can't ask why it was made or if it felt like measuring one's grave to stretch out full length along its bottom. In any case, the vacant tub, too tempting for the tide to resist, will sooner or later be taken back into the sea. Water will creep closer, a foamy edge reaching, reaching, until finally the lip of the tub is breached and the sea flows inside, exuberant, to take its own bath.

Making a gift for the sea is a compelling, involving act. Two days ago a teenaged girl spent most of the day building something in the sand. She wore wide-legged slacks that flapped in the wind as she stepped in and out of the hills and valleys she was making. I went out to have a closer look. "How's your castle coming?" I asked her as she continued to work, feverishly molding and shaping the massive construction. "Fine," she answered. "But it's not a castle." No, I could see now, it wasn't a castle. With its sinuous curves and graceful valleys, it looked more like a complex serpent mound, primitive and ingenious.

After the girl left, gulls came to investigate. They trampled the crest of the curving creation. Their footprints bore silent witness to the lure of high places, even though the peaks were only a few inches above the level beach. Soon the sea moved in. It filled the gullies and climbed the mounds. Gradually it accepted the girl's handiwork and took in her gift for the sea.

Peruvian Indians have a name for such a gift. They call it *ayni* (pronounced "eye-knee"), which means "sacred reciprocity." They believe each of us should respond with an act of gratitude for what we have. Gratitude can be expressed symbolically, as it was by the creators of the shell-studded egg and the serpent mound. It can be expressed materially, with an offering of financial help, time, personal sacrifice. The thank-you, whatever its form, Peruvians believe, should be in proportion to the blessings received. But I'm convinced that even a small thank-you is noted, somewhere, in the Big Book.

When I think of simple thank-yous, I'm reminded of Jean François Millet's painting, *L'Angelus.* In the painting, two figures stand in a field at sundown. They are surrounded by baskets and bags of grain—signs of a bountiful harvest. They bow their heads in a prayer of gratitude. Most likely they bow, not only in appreciation for the harvest, but for simple, everyday blessings. Daily bread. Shelter. Family. Friends. These subtle blessings are often the ones we take most for granted. The more blessings we have, the easier it is to be complacent.

At Christmas, I try to ward off complacency by hanging on my front door the largest orange I can find. It's trimmed with ribbons and pine cones and glitter. Why an orange? Let me tell you a story about this ordinary fruit and how it came to be on my front door as a reminder to be grateful for small things.

There once was a little boy who lived in a tiny house in need of a new roof, its lawn overgrown with weeds. Every Christmas the boy hung a much-mended sock on the fireplace mantel in the tiny house where he lived with his brother and his parents. But on Christmas Day, the stocking was always empty.

The family had little money. When he could find work during those hard times, the boy's father earned his living as a carpenter. It was a tough, cold job, and often, with a rare paycheck in his pocket, the father would stop for a beer at the local pub on the way home. Before long, he was buying rounds for the other men, and soon the paycheck was exhausted. Many nights, all the family had for dinner was a bowl of popcorn.

But one Christmas a miracle happened. The boy found *an orange* in his stocking. No one knew how it got there, but the little boy was jubilant. (Can you imagine being overjoyed to get an orange in your stocking? A Palm Pilot, maybe, or a pair of diamond earrings, but certainly not just an orange!)

This story is true. My father was that little boy. He told me about the orange when I was only seven. Even then, after having opened mountains of my own presents, it was hard for me to believe that such a small thing could create the monumental surge of happiness my father experienced. That's why, at Christmas, I hang an orange on my front door. It helps me remember to appreciate small moments: to be mindful of spring beauties blooming in the grass, sunset reflected in winter windows, and sea-catchers appearing as if by magic on the beach.

Simple things like seacatchers are often, by their very nature, temporary. Some last only a few hours. Others succumb on the second or third night's tide. Eventually, the sea claims them all. It tunnels into their dribbled turrets and pail-molded ramparts and sweeps the whole construction back into itself. But, as the woman who built the sand egg said, that's exactly what's intended.

Can we accept the idea of a deliberately temporary gift? We who restore, rebuild, remake, and
preserve-at-all-costs everything we touch? Observing
ordinary creations like simple seacatchers can be a
compelling rap on the noggin to get us to pay attention to fleeting experiences.

Recently at a local mall in my home town, the
experience of a temporary gift was repeated. A crew
of four came to work on a mountain of sand that had
been dumped just outside the food court. As days
went by, the crew began at the top of the mound to
mold images of fish and sea grass and coral castles as
if these objects existed under water. People dropped
by to watch. All of us were enchanted by this three-
story sand sculpture emerging right there in front
of the hamburger-munching patrons.

I wasn't around a few weeks later when the sculpture was dismantled and the sand carted away. I wish
I'd been there. These structures aren't meant to last.
They're as temporary as burnt offerings, sand paintings, and the wafers consumed during Catholic Mass.
The "gift" is assimilated in one way or another just
as seacatchers are devoured by the sea.

My friend Radha makes rice powder images of
Hindu gods as her family in India has done for gen-

erations. She fills a shallow metal dish about the size
of a beverage coaster with the white powder. Each
dish has been hole-punched in the likeness of a god.
When she taps the dish on the patio or front walk,
it leaves an image of a Hindu deity in rice powder
dots, a temporary offering of thanks that's meant
also to feed the birds. Like the seacatchers, in a few
hours the images are gone.

Now, as the sun slips into a dark pocket behind
the horizon, the tide begins to recede. It leaves a
polished beach that, in bare feet, feels like walking
on wet cement. Solid. Smooth. The afterglow of
sunset retains just enough light to reveal a curious
sand construction just beyond the water's reach. At
first I think it's a sculpture of a giant figure lying
on its back with arms outstretched on the beach.
Closer, I can see it's an enormous cross, crudely
wrought from sand and surrounded by a wide moat,
apparently meant to receive the sea when the tide
comes in. The only decoration on its surface is a
pattern of tiny infant footprints, made no doubt by
a very small child trying to smooth the sand with its
feet. Who has created such a thing? No one is around
to tell me.

Just before midnight, when the tide has come and

gone, I go back to see if the cross is still there. A full moon, round as a paper lantern, lights the way. It turns the sea to pearl and washes molten silver onto the beach. Outlined in shadow, the cross is still there. Except for its lower edge, nibbled away by the tide, the sand shape is largely intact.

The sea has not yet taken the rest of the cross. Maybe it has left this seacatcher as a reminder, like the orange on my door, or like the times when you received a gift as a kid and your mother elbowed you and said, "Now don't forget to say thank you."

When the tide rolls in again, the cross will be gone. That is good. Things that survive too long escape our notice, and we become immune to their message. That's why seacatchers grab our attention. By their very impermanence, they wake us up. They make us notice and inspire us to respond.

Whether they know it or not, the makers of the cross and all the other seacatchers are committing acts of "making sacred." These small acts help us recognize the value of the transitory—that nothing is really permanent. Eventually, even mountains wear down. Lakes evaporate and sometimes they fill again. Whole continents move and split. The very sand under our feet is shifting.

The tide retreats. It accepts our old work and leaves a smooth, new beach to entice us to begin again. Who can resist such an invitation? Pail and shovel in hand, we kneel to build, out of ordinary sand, another offering—another gift for the sea.

9

A Blue Heron's Vigil
Looking for Fish in All the Wrong Places

The things I thought were so important have turned out to be of small value. And the things I never thought about, the things I was never able to measure or expect, were the things that mattered.
—Thomas Merton

"Looks like he's here again," a woman behind me pipes, her voice echoing in the vaulted passageway that leads to the pool. I turn around to see her. She's dressed in a red and yellow flowered shift and wears on her head a straw hat shaped like a flowerpot. Her husband, whose torso is encased in a Cuban pareo shirt and baggy plaid swim trunks, is right behind. He carries a big canvas hamper with towels spilling out the top. They are obviously headed for a swim. But they pause, as I do, hands on the painted iron gate, to watch what's going on by the pool.

At this early hour, everything's obscured in fog. Sea and shore mingle, blotted by the opaline mist of daybreak. We three are keeping our eyes on a great blue heron inside the pool enclosure. He stands as tall as a full grown human as he clings to the pool's ceramic edge. Feet delicately curled around the tiles, his grip is as dainty as the fragile fingers of an old lady's hand holding the ear of a teacup. When he sees us, his head moves up and down in a slow nod.

"He's always here," the woman in the flowerpot hat says. "We've been coming to this place for years and he's always in that same spot on the edge of the pool. Every morning. I sometimes think, in this clear water, he expects to find a fish."

We all chuckle. Imagine showing up in the same place day after day, year after year, hoping to find a fish where there can't possibly be one! Of course the heron may not know that. But wouldn't you think that after a year or two he'd get the drift? He could easily stretch his wings and sail over the railing to alight farther out, in the shallow water at the ocean's edge and there to accost some unsuspecting mullet. But he stays. And stays.

He stays beside the clear pool, watching intently, the whole livelong morning. No fish come. No fish will likely ever come. Maybe he thinks, as he peers into the chlorine blue, that if a fish ever does come, he'll be able to see it, clear, in the transparent water. And then, snap! In a blink he'll snatch the fish in his pointy yellow bill and swallow it whole in a gulp.

"Herons have such small heads," the woman with the flowerpot hat observes. "So their brains must be about the size of a pea. Maybe that's why this one is dumb enough to look for a fish in the pool."

Well, no dumber than us humans, I think to myself, not daring to express such a thought to the talking flowerpot. I remember all my own dead ends, the hundreds of times I've looked in impossible places. I also remember the tourist families from Chicago. They used to drive the 350 miles from home, straight north, straight through to a big lake in Wisconsin. No sooner were they unpacked, than they leapt into a rickety wood rowboat and oared out into the lake, their brand new fishing poles sticking up on all sides like spines from a porcupine.

Where did they drop anchor? Right on the sandbar

half a city block from shore. Why? "Because the water was clear in that spot," they used to tell me. So clear that you could see the fish swim by. Perch and bluegill, sure. But sometimes even the big ones: lake bass, muskies, and walleyed pike. What the "greenies," as the locals called them, didn't realize was that if they could see the fish, the fish could see them. All the city folk got for a day on the sandbar was a prickly red sunburn.

These inexperienced anglers were no different from the great blue heron, except they were red from the sun or figuratively green from inexperience. Both looked for fish in places where there were none to catch. Yet they continued to fish where the water was clear. It seemed to make sense.

The real fishermen, who arrived after the summer people left, came in their battered canvas hats and faded flannel shirts and knew they had to cast their lines into deep water, into dark unseeable places. They learned through long experience that this was the way to catch fish. But even then, only when they felt a tug on the line did they know they'd found the right spot.

That's what we all hope for. A tug. Some sign that we've snagged a strike—or *will*. The heron, you, me.

We need a guide to show us where the good spots are. We need a guide with experience to lay it on the line for us, to show us the way, and to open our innocent green eyes.

These eye-opening experiences have happened to me hundreds of times. Mainly because I wander like the nearly blind cartoon character Mr. Magoo, into situations where I haven't any idea what I'm getting into. A guide usually has to set me straight.

Take, for example, the spelunking incident. I was staying at a rustic lodge in Kentucky's cave country where most of the guests, including me, were turned on to the idea of an underground adventure. Like me, most of them had never seen a cave before, much less squirmed through a tight spot in a subterranean tunnel. We hadn't the slightest notion of what we were getting into.

The management of the lodge must have anticipated our wide-eyed inexperience. Anyone who wanted to sign up for the Saturday "Cave Crawl" had to attend an informational lecture the night before. Interested, I showed up.

The title, "Cave Crawl," should have shed some light on what it was we were about to sign up for. It didn't. We forty clueless greenies arrived at the lecture expecting a pep talk about the wonders of the underground. Instead, we got an eye opening.

The ranger who addressed our group of wannabe spelunkers, and who looked far too young in his neat khaki shirt and brown tie to know what he was doing, stood before us as we sat in folding chairs under the raftered ceiling of the lodge greatroom. Despite our doubts, we listened. There was, the ranger said, a signup sheet at the back of the room. When the lecture was over, anyone who wanted to come on the "crawl" could register. You could tell by the way each of us sat at the edge of our chairs that we were already mentally headed for the signup table.

But there was one thing more, the ranger said. He grabbed an ordinary wood chair that had been shoved under a writing desk off to one side of the room. "Imagine," he said, "that the legs of this chair are the walls of a cave that you have to crawl through." There was an almost audible inrush of breath from the audience. To make his point absolutely clear, the ranger got down on hands and knees. Scrunching still lower, he squeezed himself through the narrow space between the chair legs. That was the end of the lecture. Now we knew why they called our anticipated underground adventure a "cave crawl." We filed out, one by one, past the table in the back of the room that held the signup sheet. Hardly anyone stopped to write.

We had been like the heron. We had imagined an outcome that reality failed to support. Each of us had created an image of a trip into the wondrous world of stalactites and stalagmites (although I could never remember which is which), quiet underground pools, dripped-on limestone that had grown to resemble fairytale castles. Until the ranger showed us a simulated cave crawl, we had impossible visions of it, as surreal and insubstantial as soap bubbles. We were true greenies when it came to caves.

The couple and I continue to stand, still as stones, beside the iron pool gate, watching the heron. Now, with their swim gear weighing heavily, the man flips the latch with a loud "clack" and the two traipse out onto the concrete apron surrounding the pool. Eyes wide and wary, the heron keeps a careful watch on the couple as they stow their canvas bag, pull out towels, drop them over chairs, and stretch out under a bright-colored umbrella.

Satisfied his safety has not been breached, the heron continues to stare into the clear blue water. Now and then, his neck extends and his beak goes down for a drink. He reminds me of a hollow pink plastic flamingo I once ordered as a child from a novelty catalog. The bird was a perpetual motion device. It would lower its head to drink from a cup filled with water. When its body was filled, it would jerk upright again just like magic. In time, as the water inside evaporated, the head would grow heavy again and dip into the cup for a "drink."

I watched the pink plastic flamingo for hours just as I'm now keeping an eye on the great blue heron. His feet have not strayed an inch from their original spot. And he continues to gaze into the water as if, indeed, a fish might appear at any moment.

You may have thought that my near-miss cave experience years ago would have cured once-and-for-all my tendency to imagine a skewed version of reality way, way in advance of the actual event. Apparently not. It's only after the fact that I realize life is not how I picture it. The cave tunnel is always narrower or longer than I thought.

Maybe you're like me and always making mind movies of every eventuality before it happens. In these self-controlled mental images, things always work out the way you anticipate. No surprises. You expect a fish to show up, and you sit there, forever if necessary, waiting for it to wiggle its tail across the bottom of your pond. Meanwhile, you plan. You chisel in the concrete of your mind every detail of that anticipated fish. You rivet your attention on the clear blue as if it were a crystal ball, and you will darned well stay in this very spot until what you envision shows up. Inevitably, if and when it does, it falls short of expectation, even if what materializes is a good thing.

"Ten years ago I finally got the CEO job I'd been angling for," a now-retired executive once told me. "It meant a bigger house, a Mercedes in the garage, tennis and piano lessons for the kids, membership in a country club—the whole nine yards." He'd planned every detail in his mind and the result lived up to his expectations.

Well, sort of. He was always on the run. No time for family. At fifty-two he had a heart attack, something that he hadn't anticipated. "It put everything in a different light," he said. "I realized what I thought I wanted wasn't very satisfying. Now my greatest pleasures are simple ones. I take my grandkids to the zoo, I go for long walks on the beach, and I've learned to cook some pretty tasty stuff—which makes my wife happy. All these little things

I'd missed in my hell-bent striving for success." The things he was never able to measure or expect turned out to be the things that mattered.

I wonder about the heron who stands tirelessly in his gray-blue feathers beside the pool. Maybe he is not looking for a fish at all, but merely standing still in a certain spot just like a Chinese monk in meditation, without preconceptions, just as anyone does in the emptying act of contemplation. Should we not admire his fidelity, perseverance, faith? He embodies, for us to see, clear and certain, the virtues we tend to forget in our modern, hurried lives. But who can read a heron's mind?

All I have to go on is what I read. The great blue heron, often called a blue crane by locals, demonstrates by his dogged craneish fealty, a peculiar fidelity. All over the world, I read, cranes are revered as symbols of the "diligent soul." I look up the word *diligent* in the dictionary and find a long string of synonyms. Hardworking. Careful. Steadfast. Tireless. The great blue exhibits all these traits. He hasn't moved an inch in an hour.

Male and female great blue herons are monogamous and social, I also read. They're a lot like us, or like we wish we were. Males gather materials for the nest, females build it. Both birds take care of the young, lavishing food and care.

Could we not learn a thing or two from a heron whose brain is so much smaller than ours? A bird who stands devoutly on his spot? In observing the fierceness of his glance, could we "greenies" learn to look into the sandbar barrenness of our usual way of sizing up the world and, inspired, look more deeply, with fidelity and devotion?

We as human beings don't just display a tendency to look for fish in all the wrong places. Often we don't look at all. Eyes blind to possibilities we hadn't imagined, we miss the richness we were never able to measure or expect.

When I see the blue heron in his feathered knickers and beanstalk legs, standing devotedly in his place, I think about the words of Roman epic poet, Ovid, who lived way back in the first century. The lines, which I have quoted often, explain the perverse wisdom of the heron's vigil.

"Let your hook be always cast," Ovid says. "In the pool where you least expect it, there will be a fish."

10

The Big One
Why They Fish

*Fishing is worth any amount of effort and any
amount of expense to people who love it, because
in the end you get such a large number of dreams
per fish.*

—IAN FRAZIER, *The Fish's Eye*

 People who fish don't talk much. Their
need for silence is respected by most
onlookers who congregate a few feet
behind the casting lines, content just to watch.

As one of those onlookers, over the years I've been
driven to a near explosion of nosiness. Framing and
reframing the question in my mind, I'm dying to
ask, "Why do you fish?" What I want to know is why
they stand there, ankle deep in the surf, waiting for
a nibble. And waiting, and waiting, and waiting.

Often they go a whole day without the slightest action on the other end. Why?

A few times when I've been able to gather the courage to ask, they respond with a cryptic answer and then deep silence. Is their silence a way of saying that this is a sacred sport and to talk would be akin to chatting loudly in church? Is silence itself something they protect under the guise of fishing? Is that why people who fish plant themselves a certain number of paces apart from one another at the water's edge, like gulls in their measured solitude, marking personal territory? No one is talking. At least they're not talking much.

The whole question of why people fish has itched at my curiosity for years. In all this time, I've almost never seen a shore fisher catch a decent-sized fish except once, a three-foot barracuda. Another time someone pulled in a pouty-mouthed stingray that blubbered into the sand. It flapped its rubbery wingfins until the fisherman released the hook and nudged it back into the sea. So, as far as I can tell, shore fishing hasn't produced a bonanza.

Often, any fish that does get netted ends up back in the water. "Catch and release," fisherfolk call it. But what would lure someone to stand all day on the shore, casting, only to throw back anything the line brings in? Who can understand such a motive? If, let's say, a person were to work at some gainful employment instead of casting a hopeless line from shore, that same person could buy enough fish to feed multitudes. So why do people fish?

I decide once and for all to get an answer. Today is the day. I see a fisherman in a tan fishing vest and rolled-up chinos standing near shore in gently riffled water. He snaps his rod like a whip and casts, casts far out into some unknown deep. I gather my resolve and get ready to ambush him with the big "why?" But I don't know how to ask, straight out. Every time I blurt the question, "Why do you fish?" all I get are raised eyebrows. So I decide to wade in easy.

"What are you fishing for?" He looks startled, but replies: "Anything I can catch." Dumb question. I rephrase. "What do you hope to catch? What's the best fish you ever caught?" "Snook and redfish. Caught a twenty-pounder once." This is going nowhere. He leans back to cast a mean-looking black lure with several sets of sharp hooks embedded in its plastic body. I wonder what the surprised fish will experience when he bites into that thing. I ask the man what he would do with such a fish if he caught one. "Eat it," he says without hesitation, cryptically, as if he was speaking in Morse code or cyberspeak. I'm relieved that, at least, the fish won't go to waste. But I'm not satisfied with the two- or three-word answers I've managed to drag out of him.

It was hard to believe the fisherman I spoke to was spending the better part of a day flinging bait into the water just to catch dinner. For a few dollars he could buy a whole grouper at the local supermarket. So why fish? Suddenly devoid of nerve, I shut up and move on.

I spot another fisherman farther down the beach. Okay. Start again. The stocky man in the rumpled canvas hat with fishing lures pinned all over it looks approachable. He puffs away on a cigar as big as any fish he's likely to haul in as he tends two poles, their handles held firm in short white plastic pipes jammed into wet sand.

I start easy. "Any luck?" "Nope, not yet," he answers in a fisherman's few words, perhaps trying to discourage further talk. I ask what he hopes to catch, how long he's been out here and if his fancy, brass-trimmed poles are new. He answers with "Whatever bites," "Two hours," and "Yes."

By now he's as warmed up as he ever will be, so I pop the question that's been nagging me. "What makes you fish?" He doesn't hesitate for even an eye-blink. "Anticipation," he flings back and then adds, "waiting to catch the Big One."

That's it! I'm about to hit the motherlode when another man in slouch hat and clip-on sunglasses walks up and the two men begin to talk. I don't get to ask my next question: "How big is a Big One?" Nor do I get to ask any of the gazillion tantalizing questions that suddenly begin to multiply in my head like bunnies in heat. "What do you mean by 'anticipation'? Has your wait ever been rewarded? If you caught the Big One would you still go on fishing?"

You may as well know the truth. I don't fish. At least not recently, I haven't. Maybe if I spent some time flinging a lure, tying and lying, I wouldn't need to ask "why?"

Even so, I can understand the delicious taste of anticipation that fishing brings. At grade school carnivals we used to "fish" for prizes by dropping a line attached to the end of a bamboo pole over a curtain pinned to a clothesline. Someone would tie a prize to the string and give it a tug. Up came the fishing line with a dimestore novelty on the other end. Even though the object dangling on the line was usually something nobody wanted, we were thrilled with our catch. It was the suspense, the anticipation of the prize, and especially the not knowing that made the game worthwhile. To a kid, waiting was the best part. The prize was anticlimax.

The few times I've dropped a real line, worm baited, into the water to try to catch a real fish, anticipation ran high. I never knew what I'd catch. Not knowing left a wide margin for dreams.

There are many mornings of fishing on the lake that I remember as if they were a single experience. In each of them, my brother and I and my dad (Mom didn't fish) sat on hard wooden slats in a rowboat, gripping the fat ends of long bamboo poles. We were fishing for perch and bluegills that we imagined were swimming below, waiting to gulp our bait. The hot sun began to induce a hypnotic reverie. No one spoke. We half-dozed in the sun's transfixing glimmer that reddened our ears and noses and coaxed a pungent smell of warm earth from the bait can.

Patience. Silence. Anticipation. That's what we learned those hours on the water, fishing. After a while my rear end would grow numb, and I'd grab a water-stained canvas life preserver to sit on. It was a point of honor to stay planted on the wood seat as long as you could. But no matter how hot and uncomfortable it got, no one quit the game. Like tending slots in a casino, we'd cast and wait, cast and wait—for the big hit, the jackpot. I'd watch my red-and-white bobber, waiting for it to sink.

When one of the bobbers went down, pandemonium broke loose. We'd all whoop, "A strike!" When I jerked up the line, the fish would dance around in the air like a crazed sparrow until it landed—plop!— in the ribbed bottom of the boat. Dad would take the fish off my hook and thread it, into gills and out the mouth, on the stringer in the water. Then I'd close my eyes as he baited the hook again with a squiggly worm I couldn't bear to watch being shish-kababbed.

I'd cast the line back into the water and wait. And wait. The sun melting the top of my head, the water slapping the side of the boat. Slup. Slup. Slup. We didn't speak. The mood was almost one of reverence. The few times we did speak, we'd whisper. "Will you pass me a Coke?" "Toss me the sun lotion, will you?" Most of the time I was wrapped in silence, in the thoughts of a ten year old or in no thoughts at all.

That wooden rowboat is where I learned the excitement of the suspended pause. Catching a fish wasn't the real joy of fishing. Anticipation was. The magic of light on crinkled water and imaginings of unseen finned creatures cruising by our bait down below was exhilarating.

After those early experiences, I never had the chance to fish again. But in recent years I've become more and more intrigued by other people's passion for fishing. There are an estimated thirty-six million men and eighteen million women in our country who are "hooked" on angling for the Big One—or at least motivated to drop a line in the water. When I mused to a fisherman about the difference between the number of men versus women who fish, he responded: "Women fish, sometimes, but men are really passionate about it. Read Hemingway's *The Old Man and the Sea.* You'll see what I mean."

Surprised at his recommendation, I remembered the book from decades ago, but decided to read it again to see what the fisherman meant. Hemingway, who might have been describing himself, told about an old man, Santiago, who fished alone in a wooden skiff. The old man's livelihood depended on the size of his catch, but Santiago hadn't hauled in a fish in eighty-four days. He was desperate. Yet, despite coming home empty-handed day after day, he took his bad luck in stride. "It is better to be lucky. But I would rather be exact. Then when the luck comes you are ready," the old man said.

Finally on the eighty-fifth day, luck came. Slam! A marlin nearly the size of a whale struck the bait. This was a Big One. A really, really big one! For the next sixty-five pages, Santiago struggled with the twenty-three-foot marlin, pitting his old-man wisdom and tenaciousness against the marlin's brute power. By letting the fish have its run and by knowing exactly when to tighten and loosen the line, Santiago at last manhauled his catch to the side of the skiff.

We all know, or think we know, why Santiago fished. He was a poor man. What little he earned he made by fishing. Yet there was more to it than that. Between the lines of the story, Santiago's passion blazed. His near-reverence for the sacred being of the big marlin came clear.

Though Hemingway's character may have fished mainly to earn a living, he opens the door to insights about why people fish. They don't always do it for the big catch. Or for the trophy. But sometimes,

maybe even often, Hemingway suggests, to participate in a sacred act: the anticipation of raising a living
thing from the deeps.

It's beginning to look like there could be more to
this so-called "sport" of fishing than meets the eye.
Over the past several years I've talked to more than
a dozen men and women about why they fish. And I've
read at least as many books about what drives devo-
tees to stand and cast. And cast. And cast. Waiting
for the Big One. Their motives take as many forms
as there are people who fish. But many say they enjoy
casting a line in the water because it offers an opportunity to be alone and to have a closer look at their
own inner watchworks, ticking.

Jim Shaw, a psychiatrist and occasional fisherman,
tells me why he's drawn to throw a line in the water.
"I don't fish to catch fish," Shaw says. "For me it's a
way to stay in touch with what's going on inside."
Often he says he feels a mental "nibble" when he's
engrossed in the act of waiting for a fish to bite. The
"nibble" comes as a visual image, a feeling, or even a
song that enters his head. He doesn't dismiss anything, but takes notice of whatever comes up.

"When I examine what I find, I always discover
that whatever emerges relates to something in my

life. I just let it play out as if I were angling—to get it to take the bait.

"I'm not a passionate fisherman like my father or my friend, Dennis. But fishing is an opportunity to be with people I like in ways that I like. Each of us goes into our own reverie. In my practice I talked to people all day long. Fishing is a respite. It's a way of *doing* something while participating in the experience of being silent."

Each person has a different reason to fish. I'm beginning to suspect that some know why they do it, others don't. The upshot is, the more people I talk to, the more answers I get. So far, I haven't netted the one universal response. But that doesn't mean I've stopped trying. There may be a common denominator here, somewhere, and if there is, maybe it will show up in my next interrogation.

So don't be surprised if some day when you're standing in rivulets of seawater to your ankles and casting a line far out, you look up to see someone in a battered white baseball cap with a couple of palm trees imprinted on the front. As she comes close, intent on an ambush, you may notice she has a pencil tucked behind her ear and a small spiral pad jutting from her jacket pocket. And you may hear me—uh, *her*—say: "What are you fishing for? Have you caught anything yet?" You'll know then that she's working her way toward the question—the Big One—"Why do you fish?"

Waiting for the Fisherman
Practicing the Receptive Pause

*There are oases of both quietude and renewal, and
these must be respected, protected, and given time.
One cannot force a birth.*
   —MAUREEN MURDOCK, *The Heroine's Journey*

Something waits here by the Big Water's
rim, the slender edge where land meets
sea. I come here whenever I can, which
is never often enough, to find it, knowing that if I
wait long enough in a certain way, it will, like a mirage,
materialize. I wait as a hunter waits, in the birdblind
of my mind, looking out, binoculars trained.

I sit here in the shade of an overhanging eaves,
just a stone's toss from the surf, on a chair made of
orange plastic strips. The space feels like a cave, an
eggshell of containment from which I'm hoping a

writing idea will hatch. But after a while the waiting assumes the hopelessness of a snipe hunt I remember being introduced to as a kid.

My family and I were vacationing at Shady Rest Lodge in the Wisconsin woods when I was first lured into snipe hunting. We kids were told one night to go into the woods and stand by a hole, each of us alone, armed only with a net to catch the snipe when it came out. Of course, it never did. The lodge staff had dug the holes in secret. When we uninitiated ones drifted back one by one, snipeless, to rejoin the others at the lodge, we were met by thunderous laughter. We'd been "had"!

So now I wait in tropical afternoon torpor, suspecting I'm on another snipe hunt. My pen poised, I'm ready for the snipe to stick its head out. So far, it hasn't.

Near the water's edge, a feisty white egret pretends disinterest as he stilts back and forth in the shallows. He's been pacing since dawn, waiting no doubt for his accustomed handout from the fisherman who doesn't show up. Most likely the man's wounded finger has kept him from this place where just yesterday he snagged a barracuda on a line baited with a dead shrimp. The fish thrashed up and down, crazed, kicking up sand. Then it slashed the fisher-man's finger when he tried to set it free. Now the egret teeters on its thin legs, watching out of an inscrutable eye, waiting in vain for the custodian of the baitbox, the provider of handouts, the fisher-man.

Closer in, oil-glazed human bodies, laid out like lumps of raw dough on a baking sheet, also wait. They wait to be cooked well-done, for the sun to stray past the edge of a cloud, for the no-see-ums to stop biting, for the clock hands to point straight up so they can go in for lunch. They are icons of wait-ingness. Their bodies lie flat and still as gingerbread cookie cutouts, while all around, nothing moves. Time holds its breath.

On a pink stucco wall an arm's reach away from me, a small black spider clings. She waits for a cir-cling mosquito to set down. The mosquito taunts the spider, cruising close and swerving away again and again. When the mosquito has flown far, too far even to hope, the spider continues to wait.

I think as I watch these three—the egret, the bathers, and the spider—that there are two ways to wait. The most common way is to wait for some expected out-come. You wait for your tax refund from the IRS,

for yearly vacation time to roll around, for a job pro-
motion and a raise. You wait *for* something: to get
something, do something, or be done with something.

A fifty-year-old woman once told me, "I remember, over the years, waiting to get out of school for the
summer, to graduate, to get married, for the kids to
be old enough to start kindergarten, and so on. When
one wait ended, another began. There wasn't even
an interim of satisfaction in between. Suddenly, here
I am at middle age, with nothing more to wait for.
What do I do now?" She spent her whole life waiting
as moments stole by just outside her line of vision.
Because she couldn't trust a natural unfolding, she
failed to notice the daily blessings of unanticipated
experiences.

At one time or another, we all succumb to waiting like the spider, for The Big Feast. It comes. We
enjoy ourselves. The feast gets consumed. We wait
for the next fat bug to fly by. In between we begin to
feel that something's missing.

What may be missing is an *open* waiting. It's like
dancing or playing music on an instrument. The
object is to participate, not to see who can finish
first. Unlike waiting for something in particular,

this kind of waiting is unstrictured by some future goal. It's more like what we've come to call Centering Prayer—you wait without asking for anything, without even expecting anything. You sequester yourself and let whatever wants to come, come. You sit on your metaphorical egg until it hatches, knowing that long after you're ready to give up, the new thing will peck its way out of the shell. Meanwhile, the egg must be protected and warmed.

Trusting the mystery of your own potential for hatching out shiny new may feel uncomfortable when you first try it. It's a far cry from snipe-hunt mentality where you're intent on catching a particular thing. You simply wait. And in the end, if you wait in the right way, something always comes.

This kind of waiting is an act of faith, a receptive opening. "One of the most important principles of opening is to allow what excites you to fill you up without questioning where it's going to lead," I read in Jean Carbonetti's *Making Pearls.* The trick is to wait with your mind unzipped.

When T. S. Eliot wrote that he instructed his soul to be still "and wait without hope. For hope would be hope for the wrong thing," he must have been thinking of this kind of waiting. When you open yourself in a receptive way, you allow some greater Mind to intercede. The results can be beyond your wildest dreams. Of course, they can also produce bone-crushing disappointments. But who is to say that even these experiences are not just what's needed at the time? After all, are we not, as Eliot says, waiting without hope for anything in particular?

Yet even now as the sun warms the sand under my toes, I revert to spider waiting. Suspended in a web of not-quite thoughts, I wait for inspiration to come. It doesn't budge. Instead, I snatch only fragments: glimpses of the white egret stalking impatiently back and forth in the shallows and the spider lingering expectantly near my elbow. So I wait. Wait for what fishermen here call "The Big One." But all I pull up are minnows in my mind. They are too small to keep. Trivial, these fragments deflate any hope of spearing something of consequence on the tip of my pen.

Is it possible to write about anything important in a place where, as one youngster says, "Nothing hardly ever happens"? I don't know. I keep trying. I wait. We all wait: the sun bakers, the spider, the egret. We wait for the fisherman to come and bring us loaves and fishes. We wait for what we've known before, in some fleeting moment, to repeat itself.

Yesterday, in this very place around the corner from the wind, something did unexpectedly come.

The morning is almost gone, and I'm just sitting and watching the breakers roll in. I am waiting for lunchtime and have come out to watch and listen for a while. Overhead, barely formed clouds, as indecipherable as smoke signals, scud across a vast stretch of blue that curves seamlessly to meet the horizon. What do these cloud forms say? They're keeping their puffy mouths shut. In their hurry, they nearly collide with intersecting jet trails that form a cross against the bowl of heaven, the whole scene moving slowly north, the cross keeping its shape as it goes.

Out to sea, a blustery wind dimples the water's peaks and troughs. Breakers crest into foam and leap over each other like ragmop puppies in a mad rush to shore. As the waves curl into flurries of foam, they expose an underbelly of translucent yellow-green the color of honeydew melon. Watching them is as mesmerizing as staring into a log fire on a frosty winter's night in the far north. I'm lulled into a halfway place, between here and not-here. Without realizing it, I slip into a receptive kind of waiting.

Devoid of swimmers, the water and its fringe of beach and sea oats take on the feeling of an undiscovered place. Untouched. Primordial. From my sheltered spot around the corner from the wind, all I can see is a wide immensity of green water the way it must have looked at the beginning of time. All I can hear is the groaning drone of irregular swells. Whoosh. Garoom. Swoosh. My mind goes. It rides off on the back of a long white thing that the wind shreds into foamy blips.

Then something comes. A transfixing something, like being impaled by lightning. I'm frozen to the spot. I give in. I know I can move, turn my head or flex a finger if I want to, and it will go away. It doesn't ask anything, either way. It's just there, like a deer suddenly out from the bushes and standing stark in the middle of the path. Startle it and it will run. Stay still and there's a chance to intercept its mystery.

I stay still for as long as I can, feeling its surge, knowing I'm being remade without my doing, knowing I won't walk away from this unchanged. Finally, like dissolving clouds or like raindrops evaporating from hot asphalt, the Something goes away on its own. I am left, as before, as if nothing has happened— and nothing has. The waves roll in. Whoosh. Garoom. Swoosh.

In my place around the corner from the wind, I scan the horizon looking for a gap. I wait, suspended, for the spider to capture her bug, for the egret to grab his handout. What can happen in this pause? I wait for the fisherman who has come and gone. I wait, in vain, for The Big One.

12

"Honk If You Love Conchs"
The Consequences of
Too-Muchness

*Our experiences come at us in such profusion and
from so many different directions that they are never
really sorted out, much less absorbed. . . . We gorge
the senses and starve the sensibilities.*
—NORMAN COUSINS, *ANATOMY OF AN ILLNESS*

Coincidences happen, I believe, to get your
attention. To elicit an exclamation: "Oh!" and
again, "Oh!" That's how it was this particular
morning at the beach as I was driving down
Hickory Boulevard that runs parallel to the sea. Just
ahead was an ancient VW Beetle with its paint scoured
a dozen shades of blue by salt and storm. On its back
bumper, a sign read: "Honk if you love conchs."

I had my hand on the horn, but I didn't honk. The bumper sticker was too much of a coincidence. Not a hundred yards away along a quarter-mile of beach, throngs of conchs, a springtime overproduction of hundreds of thousands of them, crowded near the water as far as the eye could see. The scene was enough to befuddle even the most committed conch lover. Who could muster ardor for such multitudes? It would be like trying to love the entire population of New York City bunched into a single city block.

So I didn't honk. But seeing the sticker did bring back the memory of the staggering mob of conchs spread out over the sand not far away. And I began to think about the consequences of overabundance.

Now, as I walk among these lumpy brown conch colonies on the beach, a rubbery foot extends from a shell, gives a shove, and the whole contraption rolls toward the water. Home free. But most of them lie huddled together in couples and small groups as if they were shipwrecked and had just made it to shore. Their huddling further weakens chances for escape. Caught on dry land and vulnerable to predators, some have tried to drag themselves and their weighty porcelain houses back into the sea. The story of their hopeless struggle is told in squiggly tracks carved by their shells in the sand. The tracks don't go far. Not far enough. As a result, many of the conchs seem to have given up entirely and lie still as pebbles in the sun.

When I see some sign of life—a subtle movement, a gray foot stretching out—I fling the smooth, wet thing into the sea. The rest I leave. Their numbers overwhelm. I'd need a bulldozer to move them all.

I can tell by their three- or four-inch size and brown speckled color that these are fighting conchs. And they are living up to their name. They continue to fight their way toward the sea. Bumping against their silent comrades, they corkscrew deeper and deeper into the sand in a futile attempt at freedom. The tide has come and gone several times since these shelled creatures washed ashore. Why haven't they floated away? Why are they still stuck and struggling?

Barefoot and tanned, a young man shuffles toward me, pauses, and stands square in his yellow swim trunks and wide-brimmed Aussie hat. He surveys the vast expanse of conchs through mirrored glasses. I can't see his eyes, but I can see the cobbled colonies, reflected double in his lenses. "Boggles your mind, doesn't it?" he says, gesturing toward what looks like an endless vista of discarded miniature ice cream cones at our feet. He flips a few of the conchs into the sea where they make a thunk! sound when they hit the water.

"They're just youngsters," he says. "You know, a female lays hundreds of thousands of eggs. The eggs hatch and float to the surface where they live for several weeks." He adds that before they develop shells, they look a lot like butterflies—and are just as defenseless. Ones that don't get eaten by coral or sponges sink eventually to the bottom where their protective shells eventually form.

Just think! A single female can produce hundreds of thousands of eggs! I'm dumbfounded. This whole phantasmagoria could be her offspring! We stand in silence, the two of us, made mute by such enormity. Of course, as the man said, most of the eggs don't survive. Still, I try to visualize the numbers of eggs each of these conchs will lay. Well, half of them, anyway, assuming half are female. Hundreds of thousands multiplied by hundreds of thousands. "Yeah," I blurt. "It sure does boggle the mind."

Then, curious, and remembering what the bumper sticker said, I ask, "You seem to know a lot about conchs—do you *love* them?" He doesn't answer right away, but tips the brim of his hat to better shade his eyes and scans the flood of brown shells on the beach. Finally he says in a low, serious voice, "I don't know. There are so many."

Is it possible to love a multitude, even when that multitude is composed of beguiling, freckle-faced conchs? They don't bite or sting. So far as I know, they're loveable. But confronted with such numbers, most passersby don't pay much attention and leave them to their struggle. Too much of anything turns the brain to jelly. Most of us can't remember more than seven numbers in sequence with any degree of comfort and, introduced to a crowd of people, we're lucky to recall a few names. Even aggressive sales people are taught to offer prospects only a few choices. Faced with more options, customers simply can't choose. Profusion causes confusion—this I remember from a story my Aunt Flo used to tell when I was six or seven.

Whenever I'd show the slightest sign of unhappiness, Aunt Flo would pat my head and say, "you poor prune!" She'd pop on her navy blue jockey cap and lopsided sweater and whisk me out to the back porch where we sat on the peeling gray steps. Here, she'd act out a story, usually the one about the yellow bandanas, complete with arm gestures and character voices. I'll tell you the story, as well as I can remember it after all these years, and maybe you'll see how the profusion of conchs calls it up.

It seems, the story goes, that there was a woodcutter who went deep into the forest to fell a tree for firewood. When he raised his axe to strike a venerable oak, an elf leapt out of a cleft in the trunk. "This tree is my *home!"* he screeched, shaking his fist. But, realizing the woodcutter was much bigger and stronger, and he, being a tiny elf, was powerless to force the burly man to stop, the elf proposed a deal. "If you will spare my tree, I'll give you the treasure that's buried beside it." The woodcutter was ecstatic, and prepared to go home to fetch a shovel. Wary of the elf's devious ways, he tied his yellow bandana around the tree so he could find the spot, later. "You must promise me you won't remove this bandana," the woodcutter said. The elf gave his word.

When the woodcutter returned with his shovel, he was aghast! Every tree in the forest was tied with a yellow bandana. He would never find his treasure.

Aunt Flo didn't explain the story when she told it. But I understood even then that too much of anything causes confusion. It's only now, standing in the midst of a sea of conchs and remembering what she said, that I realize that the yellow bandanas, like the profusion of conchs, represent the same consequence of too-muchness. In such profusion, the treasure gets lost.

The treasure gets lost when events and experiences storm over us in such quantity, intensity, and rush that we can't sort them out and make sense of them. Experiences become meaningless, disconnected. It's hard to tell what's a treasure and what's not. A treasure demands isolation—in a chest, a vault, a protectively fenced space that separates the prize from everything else.

A woman I know who's a volunteer at a local art museum found out firsthand what happens when you're inundated with too much of something—even a good something. On her first visit to the Louvre in Paris, a veritable treasure trove of art, she tried to see as much as she could, rushing from one great work to another. As a result, in the end, she felt as if she hadn't seen anything. It was all a blur. There was, in a manner of speaking, a yellow bandana tied around each of the works, and she literally couldn't see the forest for the trees.

"They say it would take four months, every day,

open to close, to see everything," she said. Knowing now the effects of overabundance, on her most recent trip she bought a guidebook and went to only one wing that held the kind of paintings she liked. "Finally, I just stood in front of a luminous Vermeer in that dimly lit room and absorbed the energy and emotion that emanated from that one painting."

To spend time with one painting, or one *anything,* draws a sacred circle within which some orphaned part of ourselves can take time to unfold. Such containment avoids the wolfish hunger for more and still more that can lead to unexpected consequences. I saw such a result acted out on the beach yesterday. A two-foot catfish lay dead in the sand, washed ashore overnight. Hanging out of his gullet was the obvious cause of death: a smaller fish, too big to swallow, that he'd choked on. The catfish, in a fit of overindulgence, had literally bitten off more than he could chew.

We're choking, too, many of us. Without our noticing, we've been marketed into overabundance. We drag our heavy porcelain houses and all our "stuff" around with us like conchs struggling to get back to sea. Gorging on too-muchness can be as compelling as a drug addiction that can't be cured by "more."

With too much on our plates, literally and figuratively, we choke. It takes more and more stimulation to feel alive.

The result is that the ability to focus on any one thing and to care about it is deadened. Too-muchness clouds experience so we don't notice or respond to the simple things that really do feed us. The soul atrophies. "We care for the soul solely by honoring its expressions, by giving it time and opportunity to reveal itself, and by living life in a way that fosters the depth, interiority, and quality in which it flourishes," wrote Thomas Moore in *Care of the Soul,* a book I've brought along to the beach. Time and "opportunity for interiority" are things the beach offers. Here we can build space for solitude. Practice it. Go inside. And, for a moment, take refuge from profusion.

What I think feeds the inner core of us is particularity. The one thing. The one thing at a time, not the ten thousand things all at once. Oodles and hordes disintegrate into meaninglessness, but a particular something, given "time and opportunity to reveal itself," can whisper in your ear like the sound of the sea from inside an empty conch shell.

Later, away from the vast extravagance of conchs,

I wrestle with squiggly word tracks on paper as I sit by an umbrella table a few yards from the water. I realize, as I try to write, that I can't remember a single one of those hundreds of thousands of conchs. They congeal into one brown lump. And writing about a lump is no small feat.

Next to me under the umbrella lies an old man blobbed out like a slug in a beach chair, a Band-Aid wrapped around his big toe. He sleeps. Now and then he blurts a walrus snort, and his wife taps him on the shoulder to wake him.

The wife, who sits next to him, has captured and set loose on the metal table top between us a pair of conchs that clatter like crockery as they attempt escape. I see that one is shiny and deep brown color shading to vanilla, the other has dull russet streaks and brown freckles. Suddenly, I feel a fondness for them both, plucked no doubt from the endless colony of their brothers and sisters on the beach.

"It's a pity they're still alive and trying to get back to the water," I say to the woman, hoping to make her feel guilty enough to throw them back. "The manager said we could take home two live conchs," she counters, saying "conches" as if it rhymed with haunches.

"They smell when they die," I add, undeterred. She turns around in her chair to see if they have, indeed, kicked the bucket. One has its foot stretched almost all the way out and is hightailing it across the table, clanking as it goes. The other seems more resigned. Perhaps near death.

The woman sighs. "Well, maybe I should put them back. The one is trying so hard. Maybe I'll just spare their lives." I don't say anything. She picks up the two conchs and scuffs in her flip-flops toward the water. When she comes back, she says, "I let them go. One of them kept trying to come back, but I threw him out again, deeper."

"Good," I say as we both settle back in our chairs, she to read and I to write in my scuba-diving Garfield notebook, stealing the conch episode without her knowing

Yes. What the world needs now is two *more* conchs. As if the beach isn't cluttered with them, already. As if it mattered that two were spared. But it *does* matter. We have grown fond of them—these two—so brave and so pitiful at the same time. We, people and conchs, have gotten acquainted, and now we know them, individually, apart from the crowd.

The bumper sticker continues to float like a mirage

in my mind: "Honk if you love conchs." If the car with the sticker were to drive by again, would I honk? Would the woman who now sits, conchless by my side, honk? Maybe. Maybe not. But at least we'll recall these two survivors, clanking desperately toward freedom on their rubbery feet. And remembering the shiny brown quiet one and the freckle-faced hightailing one, we might at least utter under our breath a small, barely audible "beep, beep!"

13

No Time for Wave Watching
The Rejection of Reverie

If we never leave our house except to drive to work, do we need to be even remotely aware of this power- ful, humbling, extraordinary and eternal life force that surges and ebbs around us all the time? Apparently not. Because we have stopped paying attention."

—ELIZABETH GILBERT, *The Last American Man*

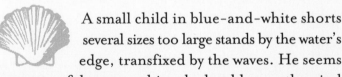 A small child in blue-and-white shorts several sizes too large stands by the water's edge, transfixed by the waves. He seems unaware of the sun on his pale shoulders or the wind tousling his fine, dark hair. The wide-legged shorts that reach almost to his knees billow in the wind, but he stays still. Enraptured, he watches the wash of seafoam as it curls over his toes.

Farther down the beach, the child's parents have walked on without noticing he has lagged behind. Father carries a plastic bag and is absorbed with searching for shells. He finds something, stoops, plucks it from the sand, and moves on. Mother plays with a chubby redheaded infant she holds on her hip as she walks. Suddenly they realize the boy is missing. "Peter! Peter!" they shout.

It takes several calls to rouse the child from his reverie. "Hurry up, Peter," the parents yell. "Run, Peter!" The boy runs bewilderedly, as if his feet are tangled in seaweed. Now and then, as he runs, he glances sideways at the beguiling waves. When he catches up to the two adults and places himself between them, each one takes one of his hands to make sure he keeps their pace. A precious moment of reverie is lost.

Disallowed dawdlings eventually will teach the child not to wonder or wander. Not to allow his mind to be waylaid by things too vast and mysterious to be immediately understood. Reverie will be short-circuited. He will give up contemplating clouds, watching ants climb a grass blade, tasting snow on his tongue. After a while he won't allow himself to be enthralled by ocean waves.

As an adult, if he's lucky, he'll realize what he's

lost and he may try to find a way to relearn how to dawdle. It won't be easy. By then, he'll likely have a spouse pulling him by the hand—a boss, too, and coworkers and friends—calling, "Hurry, Peter!" He'll have to set aside time from the daily rush to become absorbed in the sea and other things that once spoke to him. Most likely no one will encourage the clandestine commitment between the adult Peter and the child he once was.

Inside each of us, there's a Peter. We come to the seabeach, some more ardently than others, to watch, to listen, to leave room for fascination, to dawdle. But aimlessness can morph right before our eyes. Too easily, it can turn purposeful. Purpose closes options, shortens insight, and prevents aimless loitering.

Sometimes that's a good thing. If you've got a task to finish or a deadline to meet, a thimbleful of purpose could help. But don't you come to the beach to leave all of that behind? To put your mind out to pasture or at least to allow it to play with other ways of thinking?

I like writer Doris Lessing's revelation on thinking aired in a TV interview a couple of weeks ago. She said, "I think from somewhere in the solar plexus." I had a hunch that's where reverie comes from, too. So wanting to know exactly what solar plexus means, I looked it up in Webster's. I read that it's a place below the ribcage that contains a network of nerves. Sensitive. Soft. Vulnerable. It sounds like a better place to think from than our hard-wired brain.

We've always been told that it's our brains that think for us. Logically. Rationally. But could there be, as Lessing suggests, another place we think from? Skin, maybe, or heart or gut? And does this organ wish for, perhaps even demand, reverie in order to function? An accidental encounter a few years ago began to hint at an answer.

Staying at a retreat house in the country while my place is being painted, I go for a walk one evening just before sunset. The gravelly road that crunches underfoot winds among farm fields and pastures smelling pungently of grass and earth. From a barn on the crest of the hill resounds the long, low lament of a milk cow separated from its herd. Nothing else interrupts the quiet except the twittered gossip of birds celebrating twilight. And then I come upon something strange—a circular pattern half a city block wide in the grass.

It's a labyrinth, I can see now, a curving path mowed into the open field. Unlike a maze, this labyrinth has no dead ends, and leads by way of a meandering path from outside edge to center and back again. It looks simple. Or so I'm thinking in my ignorance of labyrinths, never having walked one before.

The entrance beckons and I set out, hoping there's time to complete the labyrinth walk before dark. Five minutes in, the path veers toward center, circling only a foot away. This is easy. I'll be done in no time. Then, abruptly, the way curves outward again and loops tediously around the outer edge of the circle, farther and farther from center. Not so easy, after all. I am beginning to see how the path itself has something to say, and I begin to pay attention with something besides my brain—maybe the solar plexus.

As the walk unfolds, my internal thinking machine keeps jumping to conclusions. "Okay, now I'm getting closer. Ought to take about five more minutes to come to the center. Piece of cake!" But hard-brain thinking is off by a mile, literally, and eventually it gives up in frustration. Something else takes over. Another kind of thinking—the kind that emerges in reverie— begins to open like a morning glory bud at daybreak. It blooms, I believe, in the solar plexus.

That evening, in the forty-five minutes it took to travel the entire meandering path, I discovered an extra brain that had been hidden away, like a spare tire in a car trunk. A solitude brain. A reverie brain. It wasn't rational or logical or reasoned. What was it? Searching for opposites, I looked up *rational, logical,* and *reasoned* in a thesaurus. Among the antonyms to these words were: unreasonable, nonsensical— and yes, even insane!

Is nonlogical, reverie thinking a bit, well, crazy? Roget, whose thesaurus I consult, certainly doesn't revere it. No doubt there's some resemblance between being immersed in reverie and being overtaken by insanity. Some may steer clear when they spot the connection. Reverie, you could say, is a form of deliberate insanity. You lose your mind on purpose. The difference is, you can return from reverie any time you want to.

And so I seek the refuge of the seabeach to induce a kind of temporary insanity, to become absorbed in reverie, the only state from which I can write. It's a writer's job, I believe, to stay on the edge between reverie and reality. Or rather, as Annie Dillard says, to dive and resurface a thousand times a day.

The process is a lot like alchemy. Everyday life fires the crucible. Whatever is inside cooks. Reverie is the basting sauce. It gives flavor and dimension, much like poetry, art, and music, to everyday life. When I'm in the pot, well-basted and cooking, the writing and everything else come more easily. I write things I never knew I knew. Everything flows. I go wherever the current wants to take me, which is sometimes to surprising places, places I never intended, never even imagined. Sometimes, of course, I end up totally at sea. But despite the hazards, I've learned to trust the way reverie works.

"Reverie is like becoming a meandering ant," a young woman from Singapore once told me at a conference. "Have you ever watched an ant drag a breadcrumb to its hill? It zigs. It zags. Doubles back, travels along a crack, down in, out again," she said. "For all its randomness, it eventually gets to the hill."

Okay. So maybe you're thinking that if the ant knows where the anthill is, why doesn't she make a beeline for it? Why turn a ten-yard dash into a ten-mile meander? Having no ability to read ants' minds but having watched many of them over the years, I have noticed that however nonsensical their indirectness, without exception they *all do it.* Meandering seems to be built into ant mentality. There must be a reason.

Since ants have been around more than two hundred million years longer than we have and are apt to be here long after we're gone, their meandering must serve some purpose. At the very least, the habit hasn't led to their demise. It must be that, in some way, meandering serves life.

Reverie is a form of meandering. It's a wandering of the mind in which you lose yourself and let something else take over. Peter, absorbed with watching a bubbly surge creep over his toes, had lost himself in the experience. But then he's a kid, and kids can do that just as easily as they can sit with their legs crossed on a wooden floor. They are, more so than adults, limber, both mentally and physically. Comfortable in what one sea aficionado calls "moments of delicious merger," youngsters like Peter have not completely separated from their source.

When we grow into adults, reverie often gets low priority in the hierarchy of time-takers that include making a living, keeping a house, rearing children, and the countless demands of daily life. Who has time for reverie? Probably only monks and jailbirds. As for the rest of us, we often get swept into the Cult of

Contact. We need to be constantly in touch. The cell phone commercial on TV that blares over and over: "Can you hear me now?" attests to our addiction to being reachable anywhere, anytime. Hacking through the jungle or in the middle of a vast desert plain, we must be available to fill every moment with talk.

So who cares? Isn't the state of reverie that occurs in solitude one of those unnecessary frills that can be sacrificed, like snacks from a tight grocery budget? It depends on how you see reverie: as a nonnecessity or, as the Japanese view it, a crucially meaningful pause.

A "meaningful pause" is, graphic artist Bev Kirk once told me, a way to open yourself to possibilities. "When I have a blank piece of paper in front of me, it inspires my work because it says to me that possibilities are wide open, and I can do anything I want. On the other hand, if all I think about is *produce, produce, produce,* I can run dry." Reverie is a way for her to be alone, to reflect, to develop insight into her work and her life.

The key word here is *alone.* It's a word that ought to be a verb, I read in Alice Koller's *The Stations of Solitude.* "To lone (I am inventing the verb)," Koller says, "is to become oneself and *thereby* to be able to

spend one's time pursuing one's purpose inde-
pendently of the presence or absence of other human
beings."

Being alone in reverie allows you to get in touch
with that pinpoint of authenticity that, like a light-
house beam, can direct your path. If you watch it
closely, it can lead you to the small voice from somewhere in your solar plexus that whispers, "Slow down,
Peter. Take time to watch the waves."

Peter and his family are almost out of sight, now,
far down the beach. He still dangles from his parents' grip as they walk. Then, in a flash, he slips free
of their hands and bolts, lickety-split, for the water.
Once again, the adults gather him up and draw him
along with them. But the boy has tasted reverie and
the awesome mystery of the sea, and I'm betting it's
only a matter of time before he'll chance another
run for it.

His curiosity, his inbuilt propensity to dawdle,
his fascination with all things beyond understand-
ing have not been entirely squelched. For Peter, and
for those of us who still, every once in a while, manage
to break free, there's a vast ocean to contemplate.
It's a rare opportunity for wave-watching that invites
thinking—or *not* thinking— from the solar plexus.

14

Turtle Knowing
Trusting A Secret Sense

Like one possessed, I started to inch my way toward
the truth, led only by my instinct toward the place
where the light seemed to shine.

— LEO TOLSTOY, *Confessions*

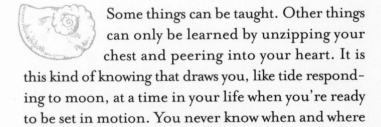 Some things can be taught. Other things
can only be learned by unzipping your
chest and peering into your heart. It is
this kind of knowing that draws you, like tide respond-
ing to moon, at a time in your life when you're ready
to be set in motion. You never know when and where
such insights will reveal themselves.

I first learned about what I've come to call "turtle
knowing" one gray morning beside the sea. There
had been hints before, but on this particular day,
the fragments began to come together.

The day begins with a raspy cackle from a crow in a palm tree just beyond my window. The sound wakes me. Outside at this early hour, fog hangs thick as the day develops slowly like a Polaroid, gradually defining the horizon where sky and water meet.

Moisture drops cling to the screen of an open window that permeably separates inside from outside. As the sea's damp presence bosoms in, smelling pungently of storm and brine, some lines from Virginia Woolf elbow my sleepy mind. "The sun has not yet risen, the sea was indistinguishable from the sky except that the sea was slightly creased as if a cloth had wrinkles in it." The words fit my drowse.

Suddenly, there's a wap-wap-wap outside the window. It's Eve Haverfield, "The Turtle Lady," part of a volunteer program to protect nesting sea turtles. I had met her several times on my early morning walks as she scavenged the beach in a dune buggy looking for new turtle nests. "Quick!" she calls through the screen. "I found a turtle nest just down the beach. Come see!"

I leap into shorts and a T-shirt, jam feet into flip-flops, and speed like Road Runner out to the beach. By the time I get there Eve is digging gingerly with a child-sized plastic shovel, scraping away the top sand, her broad bare feet stepping softly upon the manhole-sized cleared area. "I've heard people say you have magic feet," I comment as I watch her do a slow dance in her ballooning gray athletic shorts, her hair sun-bleached and partly covered by a floppy white hat. "That's because I use my bare feet to check for soft spots. They show that a turtle dug a nest the night before, laid her eggs, and covered and camouflaged the hole before her retreat," Eve says.

This morning her feet have found a soft spot. Carefully shoveling away layer after layer of sand, she finally uncovers the turtle eggs. "Look, there they are!" she exclaims as she picks up an egg in the palm of her hand. It's round and white as a Ping-Pong ball and perfectly shaped. I ask to hold one. Eve drops the egg into my hand and it feels slightly moist and heavier than it looks. It does indeed feel like a Ping-Pong ball—a marinated one that still has liquid inside. I press the sides lightly and the egg dents as if it were made of celluloid.

"The eggs are rubbery so when they drop into the nest from the mother's body they won't break," Eve explains.

I want to know how the hatchlings get out of their eggs.

"They're born with an 'egg tooth' at the tip of their beaks that helps them cut through," she answers. "The tooth falls off in a day or two when they don't need it any more."

Eve yelps as fire ants begin to attack her feet. "I'm sprinkling chemical powder on the nest now," she says as she sidesteps the ants. "That will drive the ants away so they don't get into the eggs." She also dribbles ammonia over the sand to disperse the mother's scent that could lead raccoons and other predators to the nest.

Scooping sand back into the cavity, she restores the nest to its original state and marks the spot with a post topped by a yellow ribbon. As she measures and then scuffs out the tracks the mother made from sea to nest and back again, she says, "You can often tell by the tracks a turtle makes with its underbody when it comes ashore which particular turtle this is. There are barnacles and so forth on its underside, making each one different." She says that you can tell, too, by the width and depth of the tracks how large the turtle is. Some weigh nearly half a ton and are six to eight feet across. The bigger the turtle, the more eggs they lay—usually fifty to a hundred.

Eve hops onto the seat of her dune buggy and

jumps the motor into action. "They come back to the same beach every time, you know. Sometimes they swim a thousand miles in open sea to get to their nesting place. It's a mystery how they do it," she pipes over the blast of the engine and the roar of the sea as she putters off down the beach.

A mystery. Yes. How do turtles find the exact spot, traveling far in rough, unforgiving sea, with no radar, no navigating equipment? What compels them? What directs them? And what guides the new hatchlings to scramble toward the sea? I wish I could be here to see these baby turtles struggle out of the nest. But I know it takes two or three months for sun-warmed sand to incubate the eggs, and I'll be gone by then. Still, I do remember a night when I actually saw a hatching happen.

A dozen of us are having our evening meal at separate tables in the raftered dining room of a small inn on the island of Antigua. The inn sprawls along a sandy beach at the ocean's edge, so close to the water that the shuss of surf mingles with the hushed sound of our voices. Each table is agleam with a red cloth and fresh frangipani blossoms in a hand-turned clay pot. I order crisp red snapper and chewy Antiguan bread from a menu scrawled on a blue china tile displayed on a small wooden easel. I feel quite alone at my table-for-one as conversation bubbles around me.

Then a flashlight flickers outside the window over-looking the sea. A young man bursts into the room and says something I can't quite hear. Quickly all the diners stop eating, drop their napkins, and rush out to the beach. "What's happening?" I ask. Finally, after I'm out the door and up to my ankles in sand, someone says "It's the turtles. A nest of loggerheads has just hatched!"

Everyone gathers around the flashlight beam, and I can see where it shines there is a small hole in the sand the size of a coffee can. In the hole, squirm-ing, striving to climb out, are half a dozen newly hatched turtles, each no bigger than a poker chip with legs. One struggles over the rim of the sandy pit, flippers flailing, and sets off toward the water.

Someone who is only a shadow in the flashlight's beam attempts to clear a path through a tangle of seaweed to help the tiny creature find its way without obstruction. But the fledgling wants to find its own way and thrashes straight through the seaweed anyhow. Nature will not be deterred. Or helped.

The hatchling rejects the easy path cleared by onlookers. It follows its own unerring inner radar.

I think to myself that what's true for turtles is true for us. Other people can't help you find your true course. In helping, they may point you the wrong way. You have to struggle in the direction your own instinct pulls you, as this tiny creature is doing now.

"One more wave ought to do it," a voice declares from the shadows as the small blob with its appendages working relentlessly like a windup toy, flails toward the silvery edge of the sea that draws closer with every wave. "There he goes! He's going to make it!" another voice shouts. The water sweeps up the beach to meet the tiny hatchling scrambling toward it. In a rush, the sea takes it in. Everyone cheers. It's as if each of us has, in our vulnerability, struggled along with the hatchling against the odds of nature's magnanimous overproduction to make it to the sea alive.

Later, the young man who discovered the turtles shows us one he caught in a plastic basin filled with water. Despite its disorienting containment, the wee animal thrashes about, pressing toward the edge nearest the sea. "Looks like he's obsessed with getting there," the young man says. "Amazing, when you realize he's never even *seen* the sea."

So how do turtles "know"? How do they achieve the kind of wisdom that enables them to find their way and to live longer than most of us do, to more than a hundred years? How have they managed to survive for nearly two hundred million years since the time of the dinosaurs?

For one thing, turtles are sensitive to natural forces. Are you surprised? Those leathery, thick-skinned turtles—*sensitive?* Experts say yes. They can feel a twig tickling their skin. (And they seem to like to be tickled.) Under water, their eyesight, too, is exceptionally keen. And though they have no ears outside their bodies, their eardrums are sensitive to vibrations. Most likely your thundering footsteps warn them that someone is coming and they can lumber off. Finely tuned to temperature and tide, the moon's fullness and the season, they are directed to respond to a single magnetic force that determines their direction.

We humans, on the other hand, are surrounded by magnetic forces. Modern life pulls us in a hundred directions. We're not as intimately tuned to natural rhythms as we once were. Insulated by sophisticated climate control systems, it's nearly impossible to feel the changing seasons. The Pied Pipers of our home entertainment and computer networks and the million distractions of our busy lives have further distanced us from close connection with the *real* real world.

Our focus is mostly outward, ignoring the wisdom of our senses and instincts. By not heeding our inner radar we flail like turtles without the guidance of the moon. We're pulled toward every glittery light on shore.

What would you and I be like if we could tap into turtle knowing? Not the kind of raw instinct that results in foolish decisions, but the kind of knowing that keeps you on course, through thick and thin, toward a worthwhile destination. What if we, like sea turtles, allowed ourselves to respond to what Hindus call "the knowing of the heart," a force that could serve as polestar to lead us infallibly home? What if, instead of becoming sidetracked by the bright lights of power, money, and personal comfort, we were to *live* our turtle knowing? What kind of people might we be?

Most likely we'd be strong in our purpose. The turtle heart, I'm told, is so strong it can keep beating even when it's removed from the animal's body. People who know the way a turtle knows would have hearts as big as a cross-section of a giant redwood. Their hearts would sound like thunder.

We all know a lot of turtle-hearted people. Their lives are filled with dedication to a greater cause. You'll find their names in the Bible, the Torah, the Koran—even in the headlines of the daily news. You could probably name dozens of saints and celebrities who have followed that still, small voice. But who can emulate such daunting perfection? I like to think about ordinary people, just like you and me, who have tuned in to that barely audible whisper and have made of their lives a gift.

There are, for example, the members of the Crow Indian tribe in St. Xavier, Montana. They've been inspired to build homes for the homeless out of twenty-four-inch bales of straw covered with stucco. The homes are cheap to build, warm in Wyoming winters, and look just like ordinary houses, outside and in. The only giveaway is what the builders call a "truth window" on an inside wall, a framed glass peephole that shows the straw stuffings.

And then there's Maisie DeVore, who everyone in her home town calls "Amazing Maisie." Maisie realized her tiny Kansas town needed a swimming pool to occupy the kids during summer vacation. The city couldn't afford one, so Maisie raised the money herself. It took her thirty years. To earn the hundred thousand dollars for the pool, she saved *six million* aluminum cans by scavenging dumpsters and asking townspeople to help. She sold scrap metal, wild berries she picked herself, and afghans knitted by her own hands. She followed her do-or-die turtle instincts.

Not everyone can be an Amazing Maisie. We can, at least set an example in a small way like one student in a Norfolk, Virginia, high school did. To celebrate his good grades, the boy dyed his hair blue. He was immediately expelled, because school authorities said the blue hair presented a "safety hazard" when large groups of students gathered round to look. But the boy persisted and ultimately, thanks to the ACLU, was reinstated. What if school authorities had seen blue hair as something to strive for? Imagine a whole school full of blue heads as prolific as letter sweaters, a badge proclaiming the value of intelligence and effort?

These ordinary people, the Crow tribe, Amazing Maisie, and the blue-haired boy responded to an inner imperative that drove them to achieve something out of the ordinary. They listened to their turtle knowing. They did what they felt compelled to do just as a turtle knows it must swim a thousand miles to return to its nesting place.

Don't you feel at least a twinge of envy when you consider the life of a sea turtle? Maybe there are times when you might even like to *be* one. Hang out on an island somewhere near the equator. Chow down on shellfish and sponges to fatten up for setting out to sea. Paddle like hell that thousand miles or so till you reach the nesting ground. Make love to some big bruiser, lumber ashore, lay your eggs, and lumber back into the sea. Single-pointed. Neat. Simple. No traffic to battle, no boss to curtsy to, no bills to agonize over, no groceries to haul. No stress. No indecision. Just one purpose and to that purpose every cell of your being is tuned.

Okay, so you can't be a turtle. Too bad. But you can learn a thing or two from a loggerhead. Trust your gut. Follow those positive quiet promptings. Set out on a life journey like Columbus did, despite the fact that everyone says you'll sail off the world's edge and the trip will end in disaster. You can use your egg tooth to break through to some bigger, broader, more generous life. Go your own way. Live your own truth.

This is not a pep talk. It's a road map. It's a reminder, a Post-it note on the fridge that says "Pay attention to your *turtle knowing*." You may run into some cold, rough, challenging seas. But, no, you won't fall off the edge of the earth.

For more information about turtles, consult *www.turtletime.org*

15

Broken Shells
A Passion for Imperfection

Anything, to me, that's perfect isn't too good.
—DEAN MARTIN

They say sand turns to glass when it gets hot enough. I'm watching the beach very carefully as I set out on an early morning walk. Overhead, clouds spread like an old gray quilt suspended above the sea. Batting worn thin in places, the cloud quilt muffles all but the faintest trace of sun. Even so, the heat rages on. The sea, too, appears from here to simmer. Sparkles that dance on its surface resemble bubbles in a cauldron. My wide-brimmed hat feels like the cauldron's iron potlid weighing heavy on my boiling brain. As I scuff through hot sand along the shore, sweat trickles down my chin, and my sunglasses keep slipping off my nose. But I'm not deterred. I'm on a mission.

The mission, I'm almost embarrassed to tell you, is to find a broken shell. Well, not altogether broken, but maimed, deformed, misshapen. A shell sculpted by the slam of waves and the tumbling of tides. I have been keeping a strange sort of calendar in my windowsill, made up entirely of these refugees. Every morning, I attempt to find another broken relic to add to what is slowly becoming a long line on the window ledge.

These are not Anne Morrow Lindbergh shells described in her *Gift from the Sea.* Far different from her perfect specimens of whelk, sunrise, and moon shells, some of mine are too deformed even to classify. There's one that must have been a conch shell once. Now what's left of its ivory body is long and thin like a trumpet. Another relic, its origins unidentifiable, has been shaped into the profile of the head of a seagull, its pearly concave stained with an exclamation point. Beside it, on my windowsill, I recall as I stride along the sand, lies a broken piece of freckled coral. Etched by storm and turbulence on the shell's surface is the image of a sleeping cherub, fully swaddled in her quilt. All of these fragments are by Lindbergh's standards, I expect, grossly imperfect.

Now, as I plod along, hot sun hammering the top of my head, I can see through the mist across the water the gleaming facades of Sanibel Island where Lindbergh wrote. I once tried to find the exact spot where the author conceived *Gift from the Sea,* to see if the shells were, indeed, perfect on that shore. I wrote her a note, inquiring. She responded, saying she couldn't remember exactly where she stayed when she wrote the book. So I am left with conjecture.

When Lindbergh's book first came out in the 1950s, our nation was just catching its breath after a long, horrendous war. The peacetime world that followed, perhaps by contrast, seemed perfect. Families were largely intact. Divorce was rare, or at least rarer than today. The economy had begun to soar. The word "teenager" had barely come into use, youngsters heretofore having been classified merely as children. Only about nine percent of households had even one TV, and personal computers and cell phones weren't even a blip on the screen of imagination. Yet even then, Lindbergh wrote, "The world today does not understand, in either man or woman, the need to be alone."

To be alone is to have an opportunity to shape uniqueness, to process experiences, to heal brokenness. The problem, Lindbergh mused, is how to feed the soul. She tried to help us learn how by using seashells to represent what the soul needs at different stages of life. The era of the fifties was a time of striving for an ideal world, the perfect woman, the perfect man, the perfect bungalow in the suburbs. Perfection, achievable or not, seemed a worthwhile goal to work toward.

And so I understand why Lindbergh collected flawless specimens and I collect unrecognizable relics. The times they are a-changin'. Today there's a bigger space to leap across between real and ideal. My odd, even ugly, shells are an attempt to bridge the gap by their very down-to-earth individuality, an imperfect individuality that is fast eroding in the world. My shells speak out in favor of imperfection.

But they appear to be a voice in the wilderness. The obsessive pursuit of perfection, like this morning's broil, goes on unabated. Recent figures indicate that 7.5 million plastic surgeries seeking cosmetic perfection were performed in a single year! *Seven and a half million!* These surgeries emptied American pocketbooks to the tune of seven trillion dollars. And that's just the tip of the iceberg. Think of all the other industries that depend on our addiction to perfection: cosmetics, hair coloring, air fresheners, laundry whiteners, lawn chemicals, diet drugs, and hundreds of others.

We are, Marion Woodman says, a nation intent on eradicating every flaw. It is precisely this chasing after the will-o'-the-wisp of perfection that may contribute to the rise of anorexia and bulimia, the pursuit of thinness in the extreme, she writes in *Addiction to Perfection*. Our teenagers are learning that "less-than-perfect" is not acceptable.

As I continue along the lapping water, looking for a misshapen shell to add to my calendar, I remember what Joanna Field said in *On Not Being Able to Paint*. "Beauty ought to be like happiness, something which a too direct striving after destroys." True? Look around you. See all the ways that *too direct striving after*, the obsession with perfection, destroys the very thing it seeks. And think about how this "striving after" is not just for the moment, but is a demand for continuous upkeep. Addiction to perfection becomes a permanent obsession. One facelift is never enough.

I pick up a sea-smoothed shell from the glistening hot sand and examine the graceful spiral of its tip. It reminds me of a rose I recently observed through all its stages of beauty. First, the pink bud shone as luminous as the glowing face of a young woman. Then, as the flower unfolded, it began to lose its translucence, but took on a deeper, more mature beauty. Finally, when the petals began to curl and darken slightly along the edges, the rose reflected the beauty of a woman who has seen life, experienced tragedy, given much, and earned a countenance that tells the story.

The shells in my window have earned their own stories, too. Their imperfections speak. A large clamshell, now whitened and pocked with what I call "sea holes," has three smaller shells riding on its back, each clinging like an Indian papoose. I see it as a mother shell, coddling its young. There are many others; each broken shell reveals its tale. They speak, if anyone were to listen, of the eloquence of imperfection. What I'd like to see, what I'm picketing earnestly for, is an addiction to *im*perfection. Instead of striving to be clones of each other, like Lindbergh's perfect shells, could we not celebrate our oddities?

Some do. Or have. Jimmy Durante, the comedian, constantly joked about his big nose. Dr. Phil McGraw, the talk show guru, laughs about his smooth pate. The common denominator here is humor. Some people know their flaws and the knowing makes them laugh. I look at the shell fragment in my hand, eaten away by seawater, bleached by sun, denuded of its excrescences, and I wonder: Could the shell, at some other level of hearing, be emitting just the smallest chuckle? I listen hard.

Meanwhile, I think about imperfection. I think about Antonio Stradivari, the legendary maker of the world's finest violins. Do you know what he used to craft his best instruments? Broken, water-soaked wooden oars he discovered near the Venice wharfs. He must have known, intuitively, that broken things still have music in them.

I listen even more closely to the small, warm, white shell in my hand. It may not be a loud guffaw it will emit. But I am on the lookout for any signs of singing.

And so I continue to think about imperfection as I shuffle along the dry hot sand, warm seafoam curling closer with every wave. The tide must be coming in. It tumbles ashore the remains of an ark shell riddled with holes.

The shell's destruction by the roiling sea puts me in mind of the bombed-out Buddhas of Bamiyan in Afghanistan. This pair of magnificent stone statues that once towered to 180 feet in their niches were hewn out of a solid rockface in the fourth or fifth century A.D. Just a few years ago, the Taliban, employing hundreds of pounds of explosives, destroyed the Buddhas because they saw them as "idols." Now all that's left is mostly rubble. Yet, amazingly, the outlines of the figures are still apparent on the walls of the niches where they stood. One of them, most of his face blown away, still manages a peaceful, you could almost say victorious, smile.

There is talk that the Buddhas should not be restored, though, given modern technology, it would be possible. Many think that in their destruction, in the suggestion of an outline against the stone walls of their caves, the Buddhas seem to speak even more persuasively than in centuries past. What is *not* there, what has been nearly destroyed by explosives, still communicates.

By contrast, our own attitude toward the eroding faces of the frieze of stone sculptures of ex-presidents on Mt. Rushmore demands that flaws be corrected. We are, as I have mentioned, addicted to perfection. Like faces made of flesh, the presidents' stone profiles are beginning to show signs of age. Abe Lincoln, it's been reported, has a crack in his nose. What could

be, to our usual way of thinking, a more appropri-
ate remedy than a "nose job?" Experts advise inject-
ing a plastic filler material into the crevice. True to
our national mindset, such an act would be a kind
of stoneface plastic surgery.

I am not being disrespectful of a national mon-
ument. What I'm attempting, at least in my mind,
as my rubber-soled sneakers make a trail of misshapen footprints in the sand, is to squeeze a drop or
two of humor from our commonly held addiction
to perfection.

It's well known that perfectionists can't laugh. I
am trying to point out the traces of humor in a sit-
uation and to hope for the best. I tend to believe the
advice of eighty-one-year-old artist Wayne Thiebaud
who says, "If you don't have a sense of humor, you lack
a sense of perspective." He wants people to laugh
when they see his paintings of glitzy store windows
filled with cakes and pies. I want people to smile when
they see the cleft in Abe's nose.

What can you do except chuckle when you learn
of a woman who has had countless surgeries to look
like a Barbie doll? How else can you cope with knowing that even the rocks of Mt. Rushmore are aging?
Faced with imperfection everywhere you turn, there's

no alternative but to embrace it. Flaws are what make a thing original.

At first I was puzzled when I read in *Awakening* what Pir Vilayat Inayat Khan said about imperfection. He says that spiritual maturity depends on accepting the imperfections of earthly existence, but that it's still possible to seek to embody "the richness of God's perfection." How can that be? If we can't even manage a perfect nose, with or without help, how can we embody "God's perfection?" What *is* God's perfection?

The author doesn't say. The shell in my hand was made by God's hand. Buffeted and broken, it's certainly not perfect. So what kind of perfection does God have? I visualize the cracked nose in Abe Lincoln's sculptured face, the bombed-out Buddhas of Bamiyan, and our own flawed selves. I picture the ashes of burnt everglades too dry to fend off fire, the hurricane's flood of seawater raging over the beach, and the upwash of dead fish killed by the red tide. Is *this* God's perfection? Maybe so. Maybe our culture's idea of perfection is vastly different from God's.

It could be that our human ideals of perfection are themselves flawed. All writers, artists, musicians, and others who create know that no matter how successful their efforts, they never measure up to the original inspiration. Something is always missing, or deliberately left out, or there when it shouldn't be there, or done wrong or otherwise mistakenly. The beautiful vision ends up being the imperfect reality. How shall we reconcile the two?

The Navajos may have found an answer. They weave a "spirit line" into each of their rugs. The line travels from the center, out, to show that life goes on, no matter what—even if it's not perfect. They practice deliberate imperfection to allow the artistic spirit to go in and out at will. They free it from being trapped inside a perfect work.

The shell in my hand has holes in it, holes that may also allow the spirit to go in and out when it pleases. So these holes, these flaws, are a kind of perfection. They are the way that the shell, like the Navajo rug, makes way for motion, for flow, for life. Nature's wisdom, God's wisdom, you could say, realizes that perfection can be neither contained nor maintained. Perhaps, after all, that's what defines God's perfection: uniqueness open to change. Wavewashed, lopsided, hole-riddled, world-weathered, God's perfection claps its hands and sings.

16

Taking a Cup of Seawater Home
Preserving Solitude in Everyday Life

We can't capture the storm-tossed ocean by
scooping up a jar of seawater. The ocean is the
ocean only when it is oceaning: *rolling with the*
wind, streaming with living things, pounding rocks,
fracturing sunlight, blowing our hair. The stuff in
the bottle is only saltwater in a bottle.
—PETER LONDON, *No More Secondhand Art*

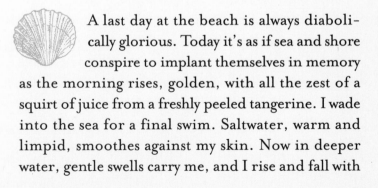 A last day at the beach is always diaboli-
cally glorious. Today it's as if sea and shore
conspire to implant themselves in memory
as the morning rises, golden, with all the zest of a
squirt of juice from a freshly peeled tangerine. I wade
into the sea for a final swim. Saltwater, warm and
limpid, smoothes against my skin. Now in deeper
water, gentle swells carry me, and I rise and fall with

them, not resisting, trying to absorb the sea as I swim. It feels delicious! The wide air above me fills with the chatter of gulls and a fragrant greenhouse aroma, damp and dizzying. My mind reels like the gulls' wheeling wings.

In the shallows near shore a blue heron begins its day, stalking on its tender feet some errant morsel. Picking. Eating. He feels like my next of kin. I stalk and consume, too. Take everything in. Sights. Smells. Tastes. Sounds. I plan later to capture them on a white page as untrammeled as a newly washed beach. The handwritten pages have grown over these past weeks to fill notebooks that pile higher and higher in my small room that looks out on the water. From here, I can see reflected in its windows the broad green body of the sea.

As a wave rises over my mouth as I swim, I taste salt. I try to remember, but even a second later, the taste is gone. On this last day I am determined to preserve a cup of seawater for my memory to sip during the landlocked months. But, like Lot's wife, looking back, I turn into a pillar of salt. The sea is already beginning to withdraw.

To hang on, I try to remember everything. I try as I once did with a hibiscus flower, to press experience between the dry pages of an old dictionary. It doesn't do any good. Experiences fade. Even moments afterward, they lose their being.

Consider last night's full moon moving like a suspended air balloon over the dark sea, leaving a path of light to mark its going. This morning the sight is nearly erased from my mind. I can't call back the scene in all its dimensions even though I recall with clarity how moonglow gave the seascape a peculiar upside-down quality. The pale silver water resembled sky just before dark, and the black sky took on the dark mystery of the sea before sunrise. But something is missing as I try to resurrect the moonwater in my mind.

Who can be blamed for this lapse? Certainly not the languid wash of waves through the night. The sound could barely be heard above the tap-tap-tap of a late afternoon's rain that continued to drip from the eaves all night long. I have not forgotten a single drop or the deep state of rest it generated. Yet I can call back only shadows. The night's remembered reality remains as tantalizingly unreachable as a rose entombed in Plexiglas.

What's left is only a ghost of the real thing. Yet I try, we all try in our separate ways, to take home a cup of solitude by the sea, bottled, corked and neat, in memory. Every night at twilight scores of people with camcorders churning attempt to seize the sunset. Poised like safari marksmen, they take a bead on the day's last blaze. When all traces of fire have left the sky, they quit the beach, content that they've captured the uncapturable.

The intent is to preserve on film what Jorge Borges calls "the intensity and tenderness of sundown." Later, the film will be packed, along with the whole experience of beach and sea, into suitcases. The lid will snap shut, and we'll think we've bagged a cup of seawater to take back. After all, isn't that why we come here? To pursue that Something that's been missing in our lives and to haul it home?

God knows, if it could be hauled, I've tried every which way to haul it. Not just a snatch of sunset or a cup of seawater, but a whole conglomeration of mementos. My shell calendars, of course, are stowed away in plastic bags, though I know full well they will molder on closet shelves at home. Snapshots, vials of beach sand, paper clip holders with seashells painted on them, will suffer the same fate.

They will be like the sea grape leaf I once brought back to pin to a bulletin board above my kitchen sink.

At first the brilliant green waxy leaf with its red veins reminded me of the short, solitary time beside the sea. But gradually, the leaf faded and it soon became as lackluster as a brown paper grocery bag. Even if it had kept its color, the sea grape leaf, out of touch with the tree, would have lost its intimate connection with the seaplace where it once grew.

I heard, a while back, about someone who collects seawater much like a connoisseur squirrels away bottles of wine of a certain chateau and vintage in his cellar. He gathers, I was told, seawater from all parts of the world. As if seawater varied from place to place. As if you could tell by looking. I wasn't able to discover how he bottled, labeled, and transported it, or what he did with it eventually. But I have imagined a number of flasks, or maybe test tubes, corked and stored in an underground chamber where temperature and humidity are carefully controlled.

Perhaps he goes down there when he wants to. Or when he needs to. And he uncaps a particular sea to sniff and to dab on his pulse points like cologne.

Has he managed, do you suppose, to preserve the live sea in his bottles? I admire any such effort, successful or not. I am hoping, soon, someone will find a way to bring home the real sea-ness without losing what Emerson calls "the wild uproar."

Like the legendary Sumerian hero Gilgamesh, who lets the herb of immortality slip through his fingers, I have been unable to preserve those rare drops of solitude of the type one enjoys by the sea, or even less, the sea itself—a small part, say a cupful. And I've not been able to leave the rollicking water behind with the equanimity Anne Morrow Lindbergh expressed in her *Gift from the Sea.* So I keep coming back to try to pull it off. To try to capture just one elusive drop. All I have are my notebooks, filling fast.

For me, something lives in or by the sea that's as necessary to good health as daily vitamins and long walks. Movie actor Sidney Poitier, born on sea-surrounded Cat Island in the Bahamas, said "I remember things here that are *worth* remembering." Maybe that's what draws us back to the seabeach: the need to remember something that's often absent from our everyday lives. Something worth remembering.

To begin to call up the missing pieces, it helps to stash away a little of what John Keats, the poet, called "slow time." Slow time is what solitude, real solitude, is made of. It's a chance to gear down to the soul's pace, matching step-for-step its lumbering, awkward, meandering ways. When you run on the slow time of solitude, you tune out of your head and into the slow reckoning of the senses. Here by the sea, the transition is effortless.

"We need to *be*, just *be*," said a little boy, who at age eleven wrote a remarkable book of poems called *Heartsongs*. The boy, Mattie Stepanek, suffers from a rare, life-threatening form of muscular dystrophy that has already claimed the lives of his three siblings. Despite his illness, happiness literally bubbles up from both Mattie and his poems, affirming the value of life in all its colors and underlining the importance of time for solitary reflection.

So I seek a cup of the sacred water of solitude to take home with me. But solitude is no more easily held than seawater in my leaky soul. I try to scoop up this morning's solitude spread round me like buttered sunshine, as a strong wind from the northeast stirs the water, as sun rises and fog dissipates, as the white monoliths of small cities at both ends of a vast curve of beach begin to glow in the early light. These two promontories and the beach between form the lips of a basin that contains, more or less, forty miles of unruly sea.

In this cradle the sea rocks—sometimes contentedly, sometimes fitfully or even ferociously. If the broad water can be grasped at all, it is held loosely in these wide arms. Enclosed, it continues to brawl with the shore, gnawing the beach bite by bite. Then, regretting, gives back the stolen sand. The squabble goes on and on. Yet the sea stays within the shore's arms, held.

In much the same way, we are contained here in the arms of the seabeach. Sheltered for a time from daily demands, we are our own islands, alone and complete. We live as a plant lives, taking nourishment and turning our faces to the sun. Solitude percolates in us, causing something there to grow and thrive.

Solitude keens the senses. If you remove the Walkman plugs from your ears, you will see better. When you take time to be quiet, to do nothing but absorb the whisperings of the sea and its salty smells, solitude takes you in. Your cup runneth over.

In such a state it's possible, for once, to pay real attention to Sidney Poitier's "things worth remembering." And, it goes without saying, solitude invites us to turn our backs for a time on the ten thousand dithers that usually crowd our minds.

"We can focus on one aspect of life, or one experience, concentrate on it, drink it in, and be satisfied." So says Robert A. Johnson in his book *She.* At the seabeach, it's possible. You can go deep. Fill your memory. Drink.

My friend Joni Powers, an Energy Therapist who helps people find balance in their lives, recommends a way to retain the beach experience, or any experience. You do it, she says, by "thinking" with your body. "You try to subdue your ordinary way of thinking and slip into bodily experience. The body has its own memory. It's not just about mental experience."

I think about her words as I paddle lazily in the sea. Lying on my back, I move my arms just enough to keep from sinking and to change direction if I want to. And I remember something else Joni said: that we know the body remembers because that's how we retain *negative* experiences, whether we want to or not. Take a simple trip to the dentist, for instance. The mere sound of the drill makes your muscles tense. The body remembers. What we don't often realize is that the body can retain *positive* experiences in the same way.

The body's way of memorizing is through the senses. When you turn off your thinking mind and focus on seeing, touch, smell, hearing, tasting, one by one, you begin to switch into body experience. Normally, there's so much going on in our minds, we tune out.

We have wisdom we don't always pay attention to. But each one of us has tapped into it, accidentally, or intentionally, at one time or another. We know instinctively that if we take time to pay attention, this wisdom can add a rich dimension to our lives. Is it any wonder we're intent on bringing home a cup, or at least a drop of seawater?

As I watch the dissolving trail of bubbles that follows me in the green water as I swim, I'm starting to wonder where I leave off and the sea begins. The sun's splotchy reflections dapple us both. Even my arms and legs seem to ripple like pale ribbons under the waves. Thinking mind has gone off elsewhere, perhaps to swim with the silvery swarm of smelt fish that dart in and out of the kelp fronds below me. I don't know. Or care.

Later, I will care. When the door of my rental car slams shut on the sea's sound and presence, I will care. Too late then, I will wish for a cup of seawater—just a cup—to take home. To use, as a woman I know does with a bottle of sacred water from Lake

Titicaca in Peru, as a healing anointment. So I search for a way to bring back the experience of sea and solitude.

Tomorrow at home my rock calendar will languish in its plastic bag on a closet shelf, far from what Emerson calls "the wild uproar." In the dark recesses of its morgue, the shell collection will go unnoticed and ultimately be forgotten. The world with its rush and demands for expediency will break in and claim what sea and solitude left behind as I reenter my frazzled life.

Once back, I know that solitude will have to be fought for and claimed, staked out like the ownership of a gold mine. Such roped-off time and space can be a day, an hour—even a minute. I used to put a blue sticky dot on my wall clock to remind me whenever I looked at the time, to take a few seconds for reverie, as Mattie Stepanek says, "to *be,* just *be.*" The blue dot helps me remember the sea, to flutterkick along its surface for a moment as I'm doing now. To feel its lift. To exult in a moment apart.

The cup of seawater you bring home, literally or figuratively, from the beach can sustain you between longer solitudes. It can fuel your creative energies, your work, and your relationships. While it's possible you could drown in an endless sea of solitude, a single cupful can flavor your life. It can, as actress Sela Ward says, "create an inner home for your true self."

This *way of being* that exists in solitude by the sea is a feeling I am struggling to learn how to preserve in everyday life. Not by trying to recreate the experience, but by setting aside and protecting precious moments of solitude.

Now as I twirl and laze in the soft, rippled seawater, I remember how playful solitude and the sea can be. Being alone without an agenda restores that sense of play, that feeling of effortless meandering, often missing from our hurried, goal-obsessed lives.

So bring, if you must, a cup of seawater home. Let it roost in your window sill and whisper in your ear: "Take time to play, to dream, to *be.*" Let it remind you to listen to the song of the sea in your soul.

AN INVITATION TO READERS

If you've come this far in *Shore Lines,* you've shared my seabeach experiences. Now it's your turn. I'd like to hear your thoughts about the book as well as your own seabeach experiences and your favorite solitary retreats, seaside or not. I'll do my best to respond to each letter. You can contact me at the address below. Meanwhile, I wish you joy in whatever solitude you're able to seize.

Mari Messer
c/o Red Wheel/Weiser, LLC
368 Congress Street, 4th floor
Boston, MA 02210

TO OUR READERS

Conari Press, an imprint of Red Wheel/Weiser, publishes books on topics ranging from spirituality, personal growth, and relationships to women's issues, parenting, and social issues. Our mission is to publish quality books that will make a difference in people's lives—how we feel about ourselves and how we relate to one another. We value integrity, compassion, and receptivity, both in the books we publish and in the way we do business.

Our readers are our most important resource, and we value your input, suggestions, and ideas about what you would like to see published. Please feel free to contact us, to request our latest book catalog, or to be added to our mailing list.

Conari Press
An imprint of Red Wheel/Weiser, LLC
P.O. Box 612
York Beach, ME 03910-0612
www.conari.com